ENDORSEMENTS

On Things Above is an amazing book: it will help every believer go deeper with Jesus through intimacy with His Spirit. This book gives solidly biblical and spiritually practical principles for going deeper in the ongoing revelation that the Good Shepherd wants to give each of us, His sheep (John 10:27-28). If you long for more of Him and more of heaven's outpouring in your life, read this book and put into practice the activation exercises. I can't get enough of this myself in my own prayer and worship times with the Lord. It has helped me hear so much more from the Lord. I am amazed at how helpful this book is.

Gary S. Greig, Ph.D.
Adjunct professor, United Theological Seminary / Global Awakening Ministries; Senior Editor for Bible and Theology, Gospel Light Publications and Regal Books.

This book is a wonderful tool to facilitate the flow of dialogue with God. If you are a beginner, or often find it difficult to hear God's voice, Murray's activations help to get the flow started. If you are more advanced, the activations will help you to jump right in to the deep end quickly. Murray's ability to train others to grow in prophetic discernment has blessed us personally. You are sure to have fun as he teaches you skills you will use for a lifetime.

Connie & Jeremy Sinnott
Associate Pastors/Worship Leaders/International Trainers Catch the Fire Toronto

ON THINGS ABOVE

An Interactive Journal

Unless otherwise noted, Scripture taken from HOLY BIBLE, New International Version. Copyright © 1973, 1978, 1984 by International Bible Society. Used by permission of Zondervan. All rights reserved.

Cover design — Jon Paul Vooys. www.vooys.ca
Layout   — Jon Paul Vooys. www.vooys.ca
              Cover image credits: Robert Michie, Lies Meirlaen
Editors   — Sally McCooeye and
              Adria Vizzi Holub. adria.vizzi.holub@gmail.com

ISBN 978-1499154832

Samuel's Mantle Publications
2582 Mount Lehman Rd #1, Abbotsford B.C. V4X 2N3

ACKNOWLEDGMENTS

To develop anything requires the ability to test refinements in the real world to see if they work. The same could be said of the journal entries in this book, and to do that took people who wanted to hear the Lord speak in community. My thanks to all the students in Samuel's Mantle throughout the years who have allowed me to refine my "listening to God skills" by practicing on them. Thank you all for your kindness, support, and belief that God is good and truly does want to talk to us.

Special thanks to Mark Virkler. If it wasn't for Mark, this material would still be hidden in lesson notes in a binder, tucked away on a shelf. Thank you, Mark, for seeing value in this material and for having the vision to see what it could do if it escaped my clutches.

Thank you, Rose, Ruth, Joseph and Kim, Dustan and Amie, Luc, Ken and Deb, Trish and Bruce, JP and Corinne, Nan and Alex, Lorraine, Cheryl, and Jenn, for helping with the classes, dealing with messes, training people to hear the Lord together, and believing God for more.

To Eric, Steve S, Scott W, Brian W, Brian H, Paul T, and Father Mike, for walking with me through the last year—thank you.

Thank you, Sally and Adria, for all of your work editing this manuscript, and you, JP, for laying it all out.

Finally, to my wife, Kelly, my sons, Jesse and Simeon, and my daughter, Delci, thank you for walking this journey with me.

And, of course to my cat Fitzimpin—thank you for keeping me awake enough to write during long nights of revision by all the scratches you gave me.

Lastly, and most importantly, to Jesus. Thank You, Lord, for walking with me and teaching me on this journey called life. I am still amazed that I am still discovering how wonderful You are.

TABLE OF CONTENTS

FOREWORD

On Things Above by Murray Dueck is an amazing book of 52 prophetic activations. I have hungered to see such a book as this for many years. It is one thing to be prophetic yourself; it is another to teach someone else how to become prophetic. Murray will teach *you* how to be prophetic.

I have taught people how to hear God's voice and see visions for some time. However, Murray has taken this a step further. He has encouraged us to ask the Lord a series of specific questions, which in turn provide us with increased insights and revelation and expanded encounters with the Lord.

As Murray points out, "We have not because we ask not." And it is the Lord's good pleasure to give to those who ask. To be truthful, I was not asking enough of the right kind of questions. I didn't really know the types of questions to ask that would unfold the mysteries of God. In this book of activations, Murray will give you a series of excellent questions to ask the Lord and by so doing you will receive increased revelation from God in a host of areas. For me, this increased my faith and has made my devotional time much more vibrant and exciting. These activation exercises have taken me to a new place in God.

For example, I had never asked the Lord where He wanted to meet me as we came together. I just always met Him walking with me along the Sea of Galilee because that is where I like to go. However, when Murray instructed me (in his book) to ask the Lord where *He* wanted to meet *me*, I was startled to hear the Lord say, "In heaven."

Murray said the next question I was to ask was, "Why?" The Lord's response was, "Because that is where I live."

Wow! An explosion occurred within me. *Of course* He would want to show me His home. And of course He has told me in Scriptures that I am seated with Him in heavenly places. Since it is clear I am already there with Him, why not meet Him there? So now I picture going to heaven on a regular basis and meet with Him. Why wouldn't I? And since Murray has taught me to ask questions, I ask Him questions as we walk through the terrain in heaven: "Lord, what is behind this door? Can we go in? Can I see what's in this room? Can we walk through this field?" Wow! A whole new realm opened up through just this one journaling exercise, and because of it, I have been changed forever in my approach to God and in where I meet Him. How precious is that!

This is just one of the 52 activations that Murray has prepared for you in this book (one for each week of the year). He will take you by the hand and lovingly and masterfully guide you into the presence of the Lord, and then instruct you in the questions you are to ask the Lord so you receive from God more of what He desires to reveal to you.

Murray, thank you for creating this gift to the body of Christ! I pray for each reader that you be taken to spiritual places you have never before gone. I believe you will be, even as I have been.

Peace,

Dr. Mark Virkler

President Christian Leadership University

ON THINGS ABOVE

AN INTERACTIVE JOURNAL

On Things Above

We are called to be Jesus' church—or in other words, Jesus' bride. And to be a bride is to be the most intimate person one can be for another. Can you imagine having a spouse you could never talk to or share your heart with? Jesus can't either! And that is one reason He poured out His Holy Spirit—so we would never have to be alone.[1]

One of the things Jesus promised us is that the Holy Spirit would speak to us, so that we could maintain our intimate relationship with Him.

> But when he, the Spirit of truth, comes, he will guide you into all truth. He will not speak on his own; he will speak only what he hears, and he will tell you what is yet to come. (John 16:13)

---

1   John 14:16-21.

There are countless ways the Lord speaks to His bride, the church: Scripture, thoughts, pictures, impressions, feelings, dreams, visions, prophecy, etc. All of these ways of speaking have been given by Jesus to his bride, the church, in order to connect to Him and to discover who His Father is. So that we, the church, can come to grasp how much God loves us. In fact, Paul prays this very thing:

> "I keep asking that the God of our Lord Jesus Christ, the glorious Father, may give you the Spirit of wisdom and revelation, so that you may *know him better."* (Eph 1:17, italics added.)

All the many ways God speaks have this purpose: to know Him better. And that is the mission of journal—to know Him better.

Biblical Principles for Interacting With the Lord

With this in mind, it is my good pleasure to introduce to you, in this first section, different ways that we at Samuel's Mantle use to commune with our glorious Father, and the biblical principles that support them. We have discovered over time, as we have walked with God as a listening community, that the Lord loves to have us ask—and He loves to answer.

> Ask and it will be given to you; seek and you will find; knock and the door will be opened to you. For everyone who asks receives; he who seeks finds; and to him who knocks, the door will be opened. (Matt 7:7-8)

First of all, we interact with the Lord by simply believing that Scripture instruct us to ask, and then, in response, God will speak. Another example of God instructing us to ask is Jeremiah 33:3, where the Lord says, "Call to Me, and I will answer you, and show you great and mighty things, which you do not know." (NKJV)

How do we ask so that we can hear? Let me lay out for you some of the biblical principles we use to listen and talk with the Lord. This is not supposed to be an exhaustive list, merely an introduction to the journal. For more biblical, historical, and practical understanding of the ways God speaks to His church, let me recommend several books to you, and websites where you can find them.

1. *4 Keys to Hearing God's Voice*—by Mark and Patti Virkler www.CWGministries.org

2. *Can You Hear Me?*—by Dr. Brad Jersak http://www. bradjersak.com

3. *If This Were a Dream, What Would it Mean?*—by Murray Dueck www.sameulsmantle.com

4. *Keepers of the Presence: A Roadmap to Spiritual Sensitivity and God's Presence*—by Murray Dueck www.samuelsmantle.com

Now on to the activation principles you are going to find in the section "On Things Above."

FELLOWSHIP WITH JESUS

To build this intimate relationship, Jesus has given us specific promises in Scripture that we can rely on when we talk with Him. One of the promises is that we would have *koinonia* with Him. In the New Testament "fellowship" is used to translate the Greek word *koinonia*, which means "joint participation, intimacy, sharing, and communion."

> God is faithful, by whom you were called into the *fellowship* of His Son, Jesus Christ our Lord. (1 Cor 1:9, italics added.)

Let's take a minute and practice "koinonia," asking and receiving, back and forth fellowship.

Having "Koinonia" Time With Jesus

- Think of a place where you would like to meet Jesus today. If you could pick the place, what kind of place would you pick? A happy place, a quiet place, a secret place, a powerful place, etc.? Take some time, ponder that choice, and think about why you chose it.

- Tell the Lord why that place. What is it about that place that would make it a great place to meet Jesus?

Stepping Into "Fellowship" With Jesus

Since we have set before Jesus what would be our perfect meeting place, why don't we ask Him what His perfect meeting place would be if He were to choose the place to meet with us?

- "Jesus, if You could pick a meeting place for me to meet with You today, where would You like to meet?"

- "Why would You like to meet there?"

(At this point, you may have had an impression, a thought, or a picture.)

For many of you, something interesting will have happened. When you asked Jesus where He would like to meet you, suddenly and spontaneously, a different place from the one you chose appeared in your imagination, in your heart by faith (you just knew it in your "knower"), or a thought crossed your mind. Where could that new meeting place with Jesus have come from? It came from Jesus—the one whose fellowship you desire. You have just experienced the first activation principle you are going to find in this journal: we can set up a two-way dialog with Jesus using symbolic language such as places, objects, actions, etc.

(Note that Jesus doesn't always change places, as He may like the one you already chose.)

Meeting Place

To start our conversation with Jesus, we used a setting, or a meeting place. Why would we use a setting as part of our conversation with Jesus? If you study Jesus' use of parables, you will come across a pattern: Jesus would use a pictorial setting to create in his listeners *emotions* that reveal what they *think* about that setting. For example, the parable of "The Prodigal,"[2] "The Rich Man and Lazarus,"[3] "The Good Samaritan,"[4] and of course, let's not forget Psalm 23, with its green pastures and quiet waters. When we picture the setting of green pastures and quiet waters, we automatically have a thought response—we are safe. We applied this same "setting creates thought" principle when we picked a meeting place. We picked a place that meant something to us because we had nice thoughts about it. Jesus also picked a setting for us, based on what He thought and felt about that setting. So we and Jesus used pictorial settings to symbolize our thoughts and feelings—just as parables in the Bible do.

Let's try to make this concept a little easier to grasp by trying this activation again, but this time adding a symbolic object.

Interacting With Armor

Let's ask Jesus for more revelation and see what happens as we step into fellowship with Jesus one more time. Let's do this by beginning to think about the armor of God, which the Apostle Paul lists in Ephesians 6:13-17:

---

2   Luke 15:11-31.
3   Luke 16:19-31.
4   Luke 10:30-37.

helmet of salvation
breastplate of righteousness
belt of truth
shoes of the gospel of peace
shield of faith
sword of the Spirit

- As you look over this list, what piece of armor would be the best for you to have on today? Perhaps you need a bit more peace, so the shoes would be the first item you would grab. Maybe you feel you need a bit more faith, so the shield would be the first item to catch your eye.

- Thinking about your life and the armor of God, if you were to ask Jesus to pass you a piece of armor that would be the perfect fit for your life right now, which piece would you ask for?

- Tell Jesus why that piece would be perfect for your life right now.

Stepping Into Fellowship

You have presented to Jesus your request for a piece of armor and let him know why you need that piece of armor in your life right now. Give Jesus a chance to respond.

- "Jesus, You know what piece of armor I would choose and why. If You were to choose the piece of armor, which piece would You choose for me today?"

- "Why would You choose that piece of armor for me?" (Fix your eyes on Jesus, tune in to flowing thoughts and flowing pictures, and write in your journal what you receive.)

At this point, you may have had an impression, a thought, or a picture.

Caught in the Act

Once again, my hope is that Jesus changed pieces of armor on you—in other words, that the piece you picked and the one He picked were different. (Again maybe Jesus liked your piece!) Why did this happen? We can have fellowship with Jesus in a back and forth dialog. We only need to learn to be aware that this dialog with Jesus may occur as a flow of spontaneous thoughts, pictures, impressions, and feelings.

As you work your way through the activation above, take some time to ponder how God spoke to you. Did you see a picture? Did you get a knowing in your knower or a sense? Did a thought pop into your mind? God speaks in many, many ways, and we can learn them all. It is good to review and slow the process down to get an understanding of how God speaks to us, so we can catch Him in the act of speaking, even when we are at work or out with our friends.

Let's build on what we have learned so far with our next activation principle.

SETTING + FEELING = ACTION

In the Bible we find another principle: the use of *setting* as a symbol for what we are thinking and feeling. This requires a response from us—an action. For example:

> The LORD is my shepherd, I shall not be in want. He makes me *lie down* in green pastures, he leads me beside quiet waters, he restores my soul. (Ps 23:1-3, italics added.)

In this Psalm, we find a setting where we feel we can be at peace. David supplies the appropriate action: lying down to rest.

Looking at Our Meeting Place

When you picked a meeting place in the previous activation, how that place felt to you probably played a part in why you chose it. We feel a certain way about a place because of what we think about a place. For example, think about Disneyland. How does that place make you feel? And what do you think about that place?

Now think about prison. How does that place make you feel? And what do you think about that place?

As for Disneyland, I am sure your feelings were joyful, free, playful, etc. Why? You probably think Disneyland is a place where you can let your inner-child out, you are free of responsibility, and you are safe.

As for prison, I am sure you felt claustrophobic, cautious, pensive, tense, etc. Why? We think prison is confined, not safe, threatening. Thus, places are symbols full of feeling, based on what we think about them.

Adding Action

There is also a third factor that influences our choice of a meeting place alongside "feeling" and "thinking," which is action. Think back to Disneyland again. What would you like to do in Disneyland? Probably play, laugh, run, splash, etc.

And now back to the prison. Consider what you would find yourself doing in that scene. Probably put your back up against the wall, avert your eyes, grit your teeth, and look for a way out! Those would be the appropriate actions if you *thought* a place wasn't safe, and therefore, you didn't *feel* it was safe. Making these comparisons and contrasts, and interacting with the Lord using picture parables, you will find places (settings), thoughts, feelings, and actions are all connected. We find this principle in Scripture as well:

> You who sit down in the High God's presence,
>   spend the night in Shaddai's shadow,
> Say this: "God, you're my refuge.
>   I trust in you and I'm safe!"
> That's right—he rescues you from hidden traps,
>   shields you from deadly hazards.
> His huge outstretched arms protect you—
>   under them you're perfectly safe;
>   his arms fend off all harm. (Ps 91:1-2, MSG)

In this Psalm, we find a place where we *think* we are safe, and David supplies the appropriate *action*: we can sit down and spend the night, we are rescued, shielded, and we *feel* protected.

Practice Time

To get how a picture of a setting, what we think about that setting, how we feel about that setting, and our actions in that setting are all inter-connected, spend some time pondering the following three settings: the green pasture and still water in Psalm 23; Jesus on the cross, and the day of Pentecost. Write down what you find yourself thinking about in each setting, how that makes you feel, and finally what you would like to do there (action). I will do one setting myself to give you an example—Psalm 91:1-2.

	What do you think	How do you feel	What you want to do
Psalm 91	I am hidden	protected	rest and relax
Psalm 23:1-3:			

25

	What do you think	How do you feel	What you want to do
The cross: Matt 27:32-46			
Pentecost Acts 2:1-4			

The above activation will help you get a feel for the purpose of parables, this journal, and your dreams as well. Often, knowing this pattern can help unlock the meaning of our dreams. (But that is another topic! If you want to dig into that, check out the iDream Seminar material at www.samuelsmantle.com.)

Asking for a Gift

As you work your way through this journal, you will often be directed to ask the Father for a gift. We can ask because of a principle given in Scripture:

> Which of you, if his son asks for bread, will give him a stone? Or if he asks for a fish, will give him a snake? If you, then, though you are evil, know how to *give good gifts* to your children, how much more will your Father in heaven give good gifts to those *who ask* him! (Matt 7:9-11, italics added.)

The Father wishes to bless us so much that one of the things He invites us to ask for is gifts. In this regard, we need to understand the symbolic nature of gift giving in Scripture. A gift in Scripture was often symbolic of what God was doing in a person's life. For example, if we think about the prodigal son returning home he received three gifts (Luke 15:22):

A Ring: the symbol of being able to do business transactions for the family, having full authority as a son.

Shoes: the symbol of freedom, only slaves were barefoot.

A Robe: the symbol of the father giving covering, honour, and acceptance back into the family.

In the story of the lost son coming home, his father used symbolic gifts to display to his son, and all of those watching, what his thoughts were, how he felt, and his acceptance of his son.

Another example is that of Mary pouring an expensive perfume over Jesus' feet.[5] In this passage, Jesus interprets the symbolic meaning of this gift and the accompanying action as a preparation for his burial.

One more example should suffice to make the point, although, this time I am not going to give you the meaning, as it will be discussed further on in the journal. When Jesus was a young child, the Magi appear with three very unique gifts: gold, frankincense, and myrrh.[6] These are strange birthday gifts for a small child, but not so strange once we take into consideration that these three gifts were given to the Son of God. These three gifts testify to who Jesus is and what he will do for all of mankind. The gifts given by the Magi are not merely items, but are symbols given of what they represent.

---

5   John 12:2-7.
6   Matt 2:11.

Asking for a Gift

Keeping in mind that the Lord may give you a picture, a thought, or an impression, begin this activation by reviewing your past meeting with Jesus in the green pasture, at the cross, and on the day of Pentecost.

The Green Pasture

• Step back with Jesus onto the green pasture, beside still waters.

• What gift would Jesus like to give you there?

• Ask Jesus why He wants to give you that gift.

The Cross

• Meet Jesus at the foot of the cross once again. Take a moment to ponder how the scene feels.

• What gift would Jesus like to give you at the cross?

• Ask Jesus why that gift. (Keep in mind that a gift can be an item, a promise, a hug, etc.)

The Day of Pentecost

• Sit with the disciples on the day of Pentecost.

• If Jesus were to give you a gift as the Spirit is poured out, what would He give you?

- Ask Jesus why that gift.

Why a Gift?

When Jesus gives us a gift, it is a symbol of how He is equipping us in that setting. Therefore, the gift we receive functions symbolically in exactly the same way as the setting principle we laid out earlier. But instead of "setting + thought + feeling = action," the layout would be "object + thought + feeling = action." It is important to ponder this concept for a few moments. Think about the gifts you received at the various locations. Could you swap them around? If you received a blanket in the green field and you wanted to lie down, would that seem like an appropriate gift and action for the day of Pentecost? If you received a tongue of fire on the day of Pentecost and you wanted to jump up and down and shout, would that seem like an appropriate gift and action while resting in the green pasture by still waters? Probably not. When Jesus or the Father gives us a gift in the upcoming journal section, what we think and feel about that object, and what Jesus and the Father think and feel about that object, will be important.

To help clarify, why don't we look at our three scenes one more time and ponder the reason for those gifts. I will fill in the gifts Jesus gave me, and a little of my pondering.

	What you think	How you feel	What you want to do
Green Pasture **Gift:** Blanket	Restful	Peaceful	Lie down & sleep
The Cross **Gift:** Forgiveness	Jesus is God	Clean/Pure	Kneel down & worship
Pentecost **Gift:** Tongue of Fire	God is with Me!	Empowered	Dance joyfully

Over and over again in this journal, the "gift question" is going to be asked for you to discover the thoughts, feelings, and actions Jesus has hidden for you in each symbolic object. This will set you up for some great pondering and back-and-forth dialog with the Lord.

We will explore this principle more as we move through upcoming journal entries.

Asking for a Promise

We all have promises that Jesus has given us as we have read Scripture—verses that jump out at us, or passages we have read that seem to speak right into our current life circumstances. One of my favorite passages is Jeremiah 29:11-13, "For I know the plans I have for you." Every time I read that passage, I sense the Lord's love and kindness toward me—and I am sure the Lord has used such passages for you as well. How can the Lord apply verses so personally to our lives?

> For no matter how many promises God has made, they are "Yes" in Christ. And so through him the "Amen" is spoken by us to the glory of God. (2 Cor 1:20)

Since the Bible is given for each of us to know the love of God, the promises of God are also for each of us; and depending on our life circumstances, God may choose to give a different promise at a different time or life circumstance.

Asking for a Promise

Once again, step back with Jesus into the three biblical settings you are working with and ask for a promise from Scripture.

The Green Pasture

- As you meet with Jesus in the green field by still waters, does Jesus have a promise for you?

- Ask Jesus why that promise.

The Cross

- As you meet Jesus at the foot of the cross, ask Him for a promise.

- Ask Jesus why that promise.

Pentecost

- As you meet with Jesus on the day of Pentecost, does He have a promise for you?

- Why that promise?

Review

Once again, you may have noticed that, depending on the setting and what God is currently doing in your life, the promise will have changed. As we continue in fellowship with Jesus, talking with Him about our lives, using symbols such as settings, actions, and objects, Jesus personally applies His promises as He knows we need them.

Journaling

Besides looking for pictures and asking for gifts and promises while we journal, we can also begin a written dialog with the Lord to unpack it all further. Following is an article by my friend, Mark Virkler, in which Mark touches upon some of the things we have worked on so far, using picturing to interact with the Lord; but Mark adds another excellent step—journaling.

You Can Hear God's Voice!

Mark and Patti Virkler, co-authors of *4 Keys to Hearing God's Voice*

Christianity is unique among religions, for it alone offers a personal relationship with the Creator beginning here and now, and lasting throughout eternity. Jesus declared, "This is eternal life—that they may *know God*" (John 17:2, italics added). Unfortunately, many in the church miss the great blessing of fellowship with our Lord because we have lost the ability to recognize His voice within us. Though we have the promise that, "My sheep hear My voice," too many believers are starved for that intimate relationship that alone can satisfy the desire of their hearts.

I was one of those sheep who was deaf to his Shepherd until the Lord revealed four very simple keys (Hab 2:1-2) that unlocked the treasure of His voice.

Key #1—God's voice in your heart often sounds like a flow of spontaneous thoughts.

Habakkuk knew the sound of God speaking to him (Hab 2:2). Elijah described it as a still, small voice (1 Kings 19:12). I had always listened for an inner *audible* voice, and God does speak that way at times. However, I have found that usually, *God's voice comes as spontaneous thoughts, visions, feelings, or impressions.*

For example, have you ever been driving down the road and had *a thought come to you* to pray for a certain person? Did you believe it was God telling you to pray? What did God's voice sound like? Was it an audible voice, or was it a spontaneous thought that lit upon your mind?

Experience indicates that we perceive spirit-level communication as spontaneous thoughts, impressions, and visions, and Scripture confirms this in many ways. For example, one definition of *paga*, a Hebrew word for intercession, is "a chance encounter or an accidental intersecting." When God lays people on our hearts, He does it through *paga*, a chance-encounter thought "accidentally" intersecting our minds.

Therefore, when you want to hear from God, tune to chance-encounter or spontaneous thoughts.

Key #2—Become still so you can sense God's flow of thoughts and emotions within.

Habakkuk said, "I will stand on my guard post," (Hab 2:1). Habakkuk knew that to hear God's quiet, inner, spontaneous thoughts, he had to first go to a quiet place and still his own thoughts and emotions. Psalm 46:10 encourages us to be still and know that He is God. There is a deep inner knowing (spontaneous flow) in our spirits that each of us can experience when we quiet our flesh and our minds. If we are not still, we will sense only our own thoughts.

Loving God through a quiet worship song is one very effective way to become still (2 Kings 3:15). After I worship and become silent within, I open myself to that spontaneous flow. If thoughts come of things I have forgotten to do, I write them down and dismiss them. If thoughts of guilt or unworthiness come, I repent thoroughly, receive the washing of the blood of the Lamb, put on His robe of righteousness, and see myself spotless before God (Isa 61:10; Col 1:22).

To receive the pure word of God, it is very important that my heart be properly focused as I become still because my focus is the source of the intuitive flow. If I fix my eyes upon Jesus, the intuitive flow comes from Jesus. If I fix my gaze upon some desire of my heart, the intuitive flow comes out of that desire. To have a pure flow, I must become still and carefully fix my eyes upon Jesus. Again, quietly worshiping the King and receiving out of the stillness accomplishes this.

Fix your gaze upon Jesus (Heb 12:2), become quiet in His presence and share with Him what is on your heart. Spontaneous thoughts will begin to flow from the throne of God to you, and you will actually be conversing with the King of Kings!

Key #3—As you pray, fix the eyes of your heart upon Jesus, seeing in the Spirit the dreams and visions of Almighty God.

Habakkuk said, "I will keep watch to see," and God said, "Record the vision" (Hab 2:1-2). Habakkuk was actually looking for vision as he prayed. He opened the eyes of his heart, and looked into the spirit world to see what God wanted to show him. This is an intriguing idea.

God has always spoken through dreams and visions, and He specifically said that they would come to those upon whom His Holy Spirit is poured out (Acts 2:1-4, 17).

I had never thought of opening the eyes of my heart and looking for vision. However, I have come to believe that this is exactly what God wants me to do. He gave me eyes in my heart to see in the spirit the vision and movement of Almighty God. There is an active spirit world all around us, full of angels, demons, the Holy Spirit, the omnipresent Father, and His omnipresent Son, Jesus. The only reasons for me not to see this reality are unbelief or lack of knowledge.

In order to see, we must look. Daniel saw a vision in his mind and said, "I was looking … I kept looking … I kept looking" (Dan 7:2, 9, 13). As I pray, I look for Jesus, and I watch as He speaks to me, doing and saying the things that are on His heart. Many Christians will find that if they will only look, they will see, in the same way they receive spontaneous thoughts. Jesus is Emmanuel, God with us (Matt 1:23). It is as simple as that. You can see Christ present with you because Christ *is present with you.* In fact, the vision may come so easily that you will be tempted to reject it, thinking that it is just you. But if you persist in recording these visions, your doubt will soon be overcome by faith as you recognize that the content of them could only be birthed in Almighty God.

Jesus demonstrated the ability of living out of constant contact with God, declaring that He did nothing on His own initiative, but only what He *saw the Father doing, and heard the Father saying.*[7] What an incredible way to live!

Is it possible for you to live out of divine initiative as Jesus did? Yes! Fix your eyes upon Jesus. The veil has been torn, giving access into

---

7   John 5:19-20, 30.

the immediate presence of God, and He calls you to draw near.[8] "I pray that the eyes of your heart will be enlightened," (Eph 1:18).

Key #4—Journaling, the writing out of your prayers and God's answers, brings great freedom in hearing God's voice.

God told Habakkuk to record the vision (Hab 2:2). This was not an isolated command. Scripture records many examples of individual's prayers and God's replies (e.g., the Psalms, many of the prophets, Revelation).

I call the process "two-way journaling," and I have found it to be a fabulous catalyst for clearly discerning God's inner, spontaneous flow, because as I journal I am able to write in faith for long periods of time, simply believing it is God. I know that what I believe I have received from God must be tested. However, testing involves doubt, and doubt blocks divine communication, so I do not want to test while I am trying to receive. With journaling, I can receive in faith, knowing that when the flow has ended *I can test and examine it carefully*, making sure that it lines up with Scripture.

You will be amazed when you journal. Doubt may hinder you at first, but throw it off, reminding yourself that it is a biblical concept, and that God is present, speaking to His children. Relax. When we cease *our* labors and enter *His* rest, God is free to flow (Heb 4:10). Sit comfortably, take out your pen and paper, smile, and turn your attention toward the Lord in praise and worship, seeking His face. After you write your question to Him, become still, and fix your gaze on Jesus. You will suddenly have a very good thought. Don't doubt it; simply write it down. Later, as you read your journaling, you, too, will be blessed to discover that you are indeed dialoguing with God.

Knowing God through the Bible is a vital foundation to hearing His voice in your heart, so you must have a solid commitment to knowing and obeying Scripture. It is also very important for your growth and safety that you be in relationship with solid, spiritual counselors.

---

8   Luke 23:45; Heb 10:19-22.

All major directional moves that come through journaling should be confirmed by your counselors before you act upon them.

Mark Virkler
www.CWGministries.org

Before I give you an example of two-journaling, let's look at one of the most famous journals of all for examples.

Checking Out King David's Journal

When it comes to interacting with the Lord through writing, David gives us some insight into his journaling method in 1 Chronicles 28:19, where he describes how he received the plans of the Temple:

> "All this," said David, "the Lord made me understand in writing, by His hand upon me, all the works of these plans." (NKJV)

We find David recording his communication with the Lord through writing in Psalm 32. The Psalm begins with David speaking:

> For this cause everyone who is godly shall pray to You In a time when You may be found; Surely in a flood of great waters They shall not come near him. You are my hiding place; You shall preserve me from trouble; You shall surround me with songs of deliverance. (Ps 32:6-7, NKJV)

The Psalm then changes to the Lord responding:

> I will instruct you and teach you in the way you should go; I will guide you with My eye. Do not be like the horse or like the mule, Which have no understanding, Which must be harnessed with bit and bridle, Else they will not come near you. (Ps 32:8-9, NKJV)

And concludes with David proclaiming the goodness of God:

Many sorrows shall be to the wicked; But he who trusts in
the Lord, mercy shall surround him. Be glad in the Lord and
rejoice, you righteous; And shout for joy, all you upright in
heart! (Ps 32:10-11, NKJV)

This back-and-forth dialog between the writers of the Psalms and the
Lord occurs in twenty of the Psalms.[9] And as it was for David, writing
a journal entry, stepping into fellowship with the Lord, and letting
Him respond in writing, is a great way to step into intimacy with Jesus.
Here is an example of a journal entry from Mark Virkler that he wrote
regarding our "Meeting Place" activation and "Armor of God" activation, which we did a little earlier in this section. As you will see below,
adding journaling to our "looking" activations of "Meeting Place" and
"Armor of God" brings a whole new dynamic.

Meeting Place

Q: If you were to meet the Lord anywhere today, where would you
meet Him? In a quiet place, a happy place, a powerful place? What
place would you pick?

Mark: I would go for a walk with Him along the Sea of Galilee.

Q: Tell Jesus why that place.

Mark: It is peaceful, and where He walked, and it is country and I love
country.

Q: Since we have fellowship with the Lord and we are told to ask to
receive, ask Jesus this: Lord, You know the place I would pick to meet
You. If You could pick the place to meet me, which place would You
pick? (Fix your eyes on Jesus, tune to flowing thoughts and flowing
pictures, and record what you receive in your journal.)

---

9   Pss 4; 12; 27; 32; 46; 50; 60; 68; 75; 81; 82; 87; 89; 90; 91; 95; 105; 108;
     110; 132.

Jesus: *I will take you for a walk in heaven.*

Q: And why that place, Jesus?

Jesus: *Because that is where I live. That is My home, the place I currently walk and the place you can walk with Me. I have much to show you about My place. Come and walk with Me, where I am at, and I will draw you into the future, into My provisions for your life. All provisions are here in My home with Me, and I want to show them to you and make them available to you. However, you have not come on up. Come on up so I can show you great things that only great men of faith have been allowed to see. You are a great man of faith. I have called you to be a great man of faith. So come up daily and ask Me what I want to show you, and I will show you great and mighty things.*

Mark: Yes, Lord, I come. This is going to be exciting. Then a song began ringing through my heart: "To Him who sits on the throne, be blessing and honor and glory and power forever." And then I prayed for God's righteousness and mercy to flow upon our president and I saw God's glory descending upon him.

The Armor of God

Let's think about that armor of God.[10]

Q: We are all in different places today, so if you were to ask Jesus to pass you a piece of armor, which piece would you ask for?

Mark: The sword of the Spirit.

Q: Tell Jesus why that would be the piece of armor you would want today?

---

10   Eph 6:10-18.

Mark: I want the sword of the Spirit so I can fight effectively.

Q: Lord, You know the piece of armor I would pick. If You could pick a piece of armor to pass me today, which piece of armor would You pick? (Fix your eyes on Jesus, tune to flowing thoughts and flowing pictures, and record what you receive in your journal.)

Jesus: *I would give you feet shod with the Gospel of peace, as well as the shield of faith.*

Q: And why would You pick those pieces, Jesus?

Jesus: *Mark, if you walk in peace, you will not need to rely so heavily on the sword. You will not need to fight. And without faith, you cannot please Me, for all who come to Me must believe that I am, and I am the rewarder of those who seek Me. Without faith, you receive nothing from me. All comes through faith and obedience. I have need of you that you grow in faith, and that you grow in peace. Put on this armor every morning, and you can lay down the sword of the Spirit to a much greater extent.*

Mark: Yes, Lord.

The Next Day

Mark: Lord, today I put on the armor You have asked me to put on. How do You see this affecting the things I do today and the way I relate to those around me? Lord, how well did I wear this armor yesterday? Did I put it on? Did I keep it on? What effect did it have in my life yesterday?

Jesus: *Mark, as you boarded the airplane this morning, you put on the shoes of peace. You smiled at people, looked into their eyes, treated them as friends, and got smiles and conversations back. The entire environment was strengthened and healed and different than when you normally enter a plane, because this time you did not see people as things, or as obstacles to overcome, but as people to love and to celebrate and to enjoy. See how much richer the experience was. Consider how much richer your entire life will be when you always wear the shoes of peace, wherever you go. That is what I am calling you to do. Now go in faith and continue sharing My love and My peace everywhere you go.*

Mark: Yes, Lord.

If you want to learn more about journaling, (its biblical foundation, and how it works), Mark Virkler has a wonderful book entitled *4 Keys to Hearing God's Voice*, which you can order from www.CWGministries.org.

CHECKING
WHAT WE SENSE

So far we have been working with "looking" activations, and have added a "writing" activation in the form of journaling. Now let's add a "discernment" activation—or, as I like to call it, "sensing and feeling."

When we interact with the Lord, we don't just see and hear, we also sense. And sometimes the Lord reveals what He is up to through what we sense. For example, consider the disciples on the road to Emmaus—Jesus walks with the disciples but they don't recognize Him until the very end:

> Then their eyes were opened and they recognized him, and
> he disappeared from their sight. They asked each other,
> "Were not our hearts burning within us while he talked

47

> with us on the road and opened the Scriptures to us?" They got up and returned at once to Jerusalem. (Luke 24:31-33)

As we read this passage, we discover these disciples were sensing something in their spirits tipping them off that they were in the presence of the Lord: their hearts were burning. There are many other examples of this spiritual sensing in Scripture, from Isaiah receiving the burden of the Lord,[11] to Jesus intuitively knowing what the Pharisees were saying in their hearts,[12] to King David declaring that there is great joy in God's presence.[13]

This "spiritual sensitivity" also occurs when we are interacting with the Lord while picturing. Often what is taking place when we sense these things is that the Lord is "anointing us" with His presence.

The Anointing

The word *anoint* means to "rub on." Think of King David being anointed with oil by Samuel.[14] But the Lord can "rub on" us a lot more than just oil. Jesus can sovereignly anoint us with peace, by causing us to lie down, as it were, in a green pasture by still water. Jesus can anoint us with humility, by having us kneel at the cross. He can anoint us with a sense of His power and authority as we sense His presence while picturing Pentecost. To learn to receive this anointing when we are with Jesus, we need to slow down and pay attention to what is going on in our hearts, as well as our heads, as we ponder and picture.

To illustrate this, let's review the armor of God:

---

11   Isa 17:1; 19:1; 21:1; NKJV.
12   Mark 2:8.
13   Ps 16:11.
14   1 Sam 16:13.

Sensing the Anointing On the Armor

Ask Jesus to spread the pieces of the armor of God out in front of you: the belt of truth, breastplate of righteousness, shoes of the gospel of peace, helmet of salvation, shield of faith, and the sword of the Spirit.

Now, compare each of these pieces of the armor not by what they look like, but by how they feel, or by what you sense they contain from the Lord (in other words, "anointed with") for you.

* Take a moment and pick up the shield of faith. Lift it high to block the fiery darts of the enemy.

Feel: What does it feel like to hold up that shield? Peaceful, powerful, strong, steady, etc.? How would you describe what you sense?

* Put down the shield and put on the shoes of the gospel of peace. Step right into them.

Feel: What does it feel like to wear those shoes?[15]

Ponder: Take a moment and think about what it felt like to hold that shield, and then compare that feeling to what it felt like to wear those shoes. Did it feel exactly the same or was there a difference? If you could tell there was a difference, what were you sensing was the different anointing from one item from the Lord compared to another?

To explore the sensing/feeling gifts to a greater degree, I recommend my book *Keepers of the Presence*. The book will explain in great detail the biblical nature of spiritual sensitivity, and how to develop it. The book is available at www.samuelsmantle.com.

---

15   Feel free to compare the rest of the pieces of armor of God to get a sense of what they are anointed with from the Lord for you as well.

WATCHING GOD'S WORDS GROW

Another activation you will find in this journal is entitled "Watching God's Words Grow," and it is based on a couple of promises in Scripture, including this one:

> For as the heavens are higher than the earth, So are My ways higher than your ways, And My thoughts than your thoughts. For as the rain comes down, and the snow from heaven, And do not return there, But water the earth, And make it bring forth and bud, That it may give seed to the sower And bread to the eater, So shall My word be that goes forth from My mouth; It shall not return to Me void, But it shall accomplish what I please, And it shall prosper in the thing for which I sent it. (Isa 55:9-11)

In this promise God informs us that when He speaks to us, His words are going to affect us just as the rain and snow would affect a crop—plants grow and mature as a result of rain! In the same way, God's words will affect us, and, over time, we are going to grow and become spiritually mature. But Isaiah 55:10 tells us that sprouting is not all a plant does: in time, it also produces seed for the sower and bread for the eater. Eventually we will have seed to give away and bread for others to eat. In other words, these words of God will produce so much good growth in our lives we will have tons of God's love and life to give away to others!

Let's look at a New Testament verse that parallels this growth principle.

> However, when He, the Spirit of truth, has come, He will guide you into all truth; for He will not speak on His own authority, but whatever He hears He will speak; and He will tell you things to come. (John 16:13, NKJV)

Here we find Jesus making us a promise that the Holy Spirit will talk to us about our future. Put simply, we have permission to ask the Lord to show us how we will spiritually mature over time as His words impact us.

Let's give it a try and see what happens.

Learning To Watch Seed Grow

- Step back with the Lord into that green pasture beside still water. Take a moment to picture the scene. What does it feel like to be there? What do you sense?

Now that you are with Jesus in this place of rest, ask Him a question.

- "Lord if I keep meeting You here in this place of rest and peace, day after day, month after month, year after year, what is going to grow in my life? What is going to change and develop? Lord, could you fast-forward this picture one year, two years, five years? What is going to change if I keep meeting You in this place of rest?" (Fix your eyes on Jesus, tune to flowing thoughts and flowing pictures, and record what you receive in your journal.)

What changed for you as you stepped into fellowship with the Lord and asked that question? Did the picture change? Did you get a sense of personal growth? Perhaps you felt the joy of the Lord as He sees you becoming all you can be. Any of these would be great (and I am sure there are many other things the Lord could have shown you or told you, as well).

Try this activation again, but this time with the armor of God you received earlier. Think about that piece of armor God gave you and ask the same question:

• "Lord, if I value this piece of the armor and learn to use it day after day, month after month, year after year, what is going to grow in my life; what is going to change and develop? Lord could you fast-forward this picture a year, two years, five years?" (Fix your eyes on Jesus, tune to flowing thoughts and flowing pictures, and record what you receive in your journal.)

Once again, take note of any changes or new thoughts, feelings, or pictures the Lord gave you.

THE LORD'S PERSPECTIVE

As we journal with the Lord and have fellowship with Him, there is another promise in Scripture we can access:

> For who among men knows the *thoughts* of a man except the man's spirit within him? In the same way no one knows the *thoughts of God* except the Spirit of God. We have not received the spirit of the world but the Spirit who is from God, that we may *understand* what God has freely given us. (1 Cor 2:11-12, italics added.)

Wouldn't it be wonderful to be able to access what God thinks and feels about what is going on in our lives or in the lives of the people we love? We can do this very thing because:

> For "who has known the mind of the Lord that he may instruct Him?" But we have the mind of Christ. (1 Cor 2:16)

As a result of receiving the Spirit of God, we can access what Jesus wants us to know about what He is thinking and feeling. To do so, we need to take Him up on His offer in John 15:4 to, "abide in Me, and I in you." To *abide* means to "live in, connect to, remain in." Jesus states this same principle in another way:

> At that day you will know that I am in My Father, and you in Me, and I in you. (John 14:20)

To activate this promise and receive the mind of Christ, all we need to do is take Jesus up on His offer to be in Him, and He in us.

Stepping Into Jesus' Shoes

I propose doing this activation two different ways, as my desire at this point is for you to clearly see that what you think of a person or situation may be quite different from what the Lord thinks. If we can clearly differentiate between your thinking and the Lord's, it will help you as you move through the activations further along in this journal.

- Think of someone you are struggling with right now, someone about whom it takes a bit of an effort to think kind thoughts. You may have very valid reasons for feeling as you do; perhaps this person has not honored you as you should be honored. That being the case, Jesus can help you find peace in this situation by giving you His thoughts. Therefore, try this:

- Picture a place where you are with this person (that may be at home, work, church, etc.).

- Invite Jesus to come and meet you in this scene. Look to see where Jesus would sit, stand, or kneel.

- Take a moment and tell Jesus how you are feeling about this person, including feelings of conflict.

You have presented this person and any conflict involving them to Jesus as well as how you are thinking and feeling about them and the situation. Now change perspective: look at this person from Jesus' point of view.

- "Jesus, when you look at this person, what do You see, think, and feel? Would You allow me to see this person from Your point of view?"

Helpful Hint: If you don't receive anything new from Jesus right away, try this helpful prophetic act: in your picture with Jesus and this person, walk over to Jesus and step right into Him. (As the scripture stated earlier, be "in Him.") As you are standing in Jesus, look at this person through Jesus' eyes. Be aware of any differences between what you see regarding this person and what Jesus sees. This little extra step will assist you to receive Jesus' point of view and allow you to feel what He feels and think what He thinks.

Review

Take a few moments to compare and contrast what you saw, thought, and felt when looking at this person, and what Jesus saw, thought, and felt. What did the Holy Spirit reveal to you that you hadn't thought of before?

The reason I included the last activation is that Jesus is never worried, anxious, or fearful—even if we are. Therefore, quite often, it is easier to catch the difference between what we are thinking and what the Lord is thinking if our thoughts are negative while His are restful. Nevertheless, so that we don't end on a negative note, let's try this following activation as well:

Observing the Joy of Lord

- Begin by picturing a meeting with Jesus in that green pasture, by that still water. Spend a few moments being with Jesus, our Good Shepherd. Pay attention to where Jesus would stand, sit, or kneel.

- Think of someone who has really grown in the Lord over the last number of years—someone in whom the inner work of the Holy Spirit has been really obvious. Ask Jesus to add this person into your picture of the green pasture and still water. Where would Jesus like this person to sit or stand?

Now that the scene includes the person who has really grown in the Lord, walk over to the Lord and step into Him again. Ask the Lord to give you the mind of Christ so that, as you look through His eyes, He can show you what He sees, thinks, and feels when He looks at this person.

Once again, compare what you saw, thought, and felt to what the Lord saw, thought, and felt. Be aware that since both you and Lord affirmed the person's growth, you may or may not have seen exactly the same thing. Take some time with Jesus and ask Him why He views this person the way He does.

Review

The thought of being in Christ and He being in us will definitely require a bit of getting used to. You may want to practice the above two activations a few times, using different people as examples. Hopefully, the two activations above will help you catch the power in this promise of the Lord to access the mind of Christ. Also, these two activations are effective ways to figure out how to pray for someone, in accordance with God's will.

There are quite a few other biblical principles dealing with dialoging with the Lord that are given in *On Things Above*, but I will let you work your way through them as you journal with the Lord.

Now let's take time to talk about the process of testing revelation, before you begin using the journal.

TESTING REVELATION

Finally, a word about testing. I am fond of telling my classes that to be a Christian, we must test revelation. But, according to 1 Thessalonians 5:19-21, testing is third on the priority list:

[1] Do not quench the Spirit.
[2] Do not despise prophecies.
[3] Test all things;
[4] Hold fast [to] what is good.

To grasp what Paul is trying to communicate to us, think of it like this:

- You have been waiting to go on a date with someone for weeks, but when the big day finally arrives, your date is three hours late—and doesn't even apologize! You could say that your expectations for that date were quenched.

61

- Then, when you finally go out on the date, this person you have been waiting to talk to all week only talks about himself/herself the whole time and makes no room for you to express yourself! You could say that your voice had been despised.

- At the end of it all, you're going to need to test the whole experience. Do you really want to go out with this person again?

This is the same order in which we need to proceed when we are having fellowship with our beloved Jesus, by the Holy Spirit. We want to honour being with Him; listen to Him; and then, at the end of the time, test it all, hanging on to what is authentic. If Jesus is speaking to us, then what we are hearing must line up with what He has already revealed about His character and ways in the Bible. Jesus is not going to contradict Himself.

We need to test any revelation with:

Scripture: What does the Bible say about what you are hearing? Second Timothy 3:16 says, "All scripture is God breathed and profitable for right doctrine and training in righteousness." We need to know what the Bible says.

Fruit: Galatians 5:22-23 informs us that the fruit of the Holy Spirit is love, joy, peace, longsuffering, kindness, goodness, faithfulness, gentleness, and self-control. The gifts of the Spirit must produce the fruit of the Spirit. What does the revelation you have received produce in you? What would be the fruit of believing and following what you heard?

Inner Witness: How do you personally feel about the revelation you have received? Sometimes it is easy to convince ourselves that something is right, even though we feel a check. What do you sense in your spirit?

The Body: Take what you have received and bounce it off three other people. Scripture talks about how everything is confirmed by two or three witnesses.[16] Find a few people with a track record of hearing God's voice and having good character, and share with them what you have received. Prophecy is a team sport—include your team.

Confirmation: If the Lord has spoken to you, He will speak again and again through multiple sources: scripture, sermons, friends, music, dreams, prophecy, etc. Record all you have received, and then keep your eyes and ears open for God to keep speaking to you.

---

16   Matt 18:16.

Preparing To Encounter the Lord

Before we begin our journey with the journal, we should take one last moment and talk a little about preparation. You will need a Bible, pen, some paper, and a quiet space to be. The most important preparation, however, is the preparation of your heart. You can tune your heart to the Lord while listening to worship music, being in worshipful stillness, spending some time reading Scripture, or even just talking to Jesus about your day. Whatever works for you in order to come into the arms of your Father and feel loved, cared for, and valued is the right thing to do. That may include all of the above, and many other ways besides.

One final note concerning the journal you are holding: its purpose is to draw you into intimacy with the Lord, and that involves talking and spending time together. So take a deep breath, slow down, stop when you want to, skip things and come back, take sections out of order, repeat your favorite parts again and again—this is not a race to complete, but a relationship to invest in. Feel free to stay on certain journal entries for weeks, pondering them with Jesus. Other entries, you might do in a few minutes. Whatever you do, do what feels right and works for you. Some of you will picture more, some will write back-and-forth with the Lord more, and some will sense or feel more strongly. We can look forward to growing in all of these areas of gifting as we walk through the pages of this journal together with Jesus.

Regarding the development of your own style, you will find at the back of this book a series of journal entries from *On Things Above*, worked through by different people from Samuel's Mantle. I hope this will give you some idea of how to develop your own journal entries with Jesus; it will be a little different for everyone. Please read them all, test them with the tests provided, and observe how the different writers interacted with the journal entries as they were led by the Spirit. You will notice that they all developed their own unique style and methods. Hopefully this will help you get a feel for how the Lord will meet you as you interact with Jesus through the pages of this little book.

With all of this in mind let's begin our journey of journaling with the Lord by setting our mind and hearts on things above.[17]

---

17   Col 3:1-2.

ACTIVATIONS

Week 1

THE BOOK

Have you ever wanted to find out what was written about you in someone's journal, possibly to find out what was secretly said about you? What was your heart looking for? Connection, love, understanding, affirmation, intimacy—perhaps all of the above? God loves that inquisitive excitement, or at least when it comes to peeking into one particular journal book: His journal of our lives.

> All the days ordained for me were written in your book before one of them came to be. How precious to me are your thoughts, O God! How vast is the sum of them! Were I to count them, they would outnumber the grains of sand. (Ps 139:16-18)

It may be surprising that God has a personal journal too, a book He keeps about the highlights of our lives. It contains the story of our creation, with our highs and lows, our hopes and dreams. It is a book that outlines our days and, more importantly, records the thoughts of the Lord towards us. These thoughts are more numerous than all the grains of sand.

The Father's Heavenly Journal

Books are quite individual things. I tend to like journals that feel old, heavy, and have symbols of some form on them—it just feels right. Others like their journals covered with pictures of flowers or musical notes. To each his own. But what of the Lord's journal of your life? How would its cover look? Ask Jesus to pull out the journal of your life so you can take a good look at it.

Look: Is the Lord's journal about your life big or small?

Q: If there were precious stones on the cover and the binding of your journal, what colors would they be?

Q: Ask Jesus why those colors.

Q: How about symbols such as the cross, musical notes, or a sword? Look to see what symbols the Lord would place on your journal. And ask Jesus why those symbols.

Look: As Jesus reveals this journal to you, what is the expression on His face?

Q: Ask the Lord why He has that expression.

Journal what the Lord shows you and ask Him about this marvelous book. Talk with Him about it.

Week 2

Taking a Look Inside the Book

For no matter how many promises God has made, they are
"Yes" in Christ. And so through him the "Amen" is spoken by
us to the glory of God. (2 Cor 1:20)

Since books are made to be read, and the Lord loves giving us promises
about our lives, the time has come for you to ask Jesus to open His
journal so you can take a peek inside.

Q: If all God's promises are "yes" to us, think about your life, written in
this book. If there was a life verse that would encapsulate your journey
with Jesus—a verse that, if we flipped the book open, we would find on
the first page—what would it be?

Look and listen to see what it would be.

Q: Ask Jesus why that verse is so important.

Journal what God has shown you and told you.

Chapter and Verse

As you think about this promise of God over your life, there may be an
event that exemplifies the reason Jesus put that verse in your journal.

Q: If God could flip open the journal about your life and have it open to a particular chapter which He cherishes, what would it be? What was happening at that time in your life?

Q: Ask the Lord why He picked that chapter.

Look: "Jesus, would you show me what You were doing in my life at that time?" Now, picture that scene of your life again (or get a sense of it), invite Jesus in, and watch what He did for you.

Q: "Jesus, as I watched what you were doing, please tell me why You did that."

Journal anything the Lord showed you or told you, and talk with Him about it.

Final thought: It is possible that the chapter God has highlighted may change from time to time, as God wants you to review different aspects of your life with Him. Come back, sit with the Lord, and peer into the book often; you may be surprised that God cherishes things about your life you may have even forgotten about or took no notice of.

Week 3

COUNTING THE COST

The kingdom of heaven is like treasure hidden in a field. When a man found it, he hid it again, and then in his joy went and sold all he had and bought that field. (Matt 13:44)

When I was a teenager, I was in love with a motorcycle. I had never wanted anything so much! I begged and pleaded with my dad for that motorcycle, but, to my chagrin, my dad wanted to make me a deal: if I would earn half the money for that bike, he would cover the other half. The moral outrage—the betrayal! How could he do this to me? I would never be able to come up with that kind of money! But, little by little, through delivering papers and working on Saturdays, I managed it. And I will never forget the joy of walking into that store one day and wheeling out my brand new motorcycle.

As I drove that motorcycle through the fields that afternoon, I discovered something: I valued that machine so much more because it had cost me something—just like the kingdom of heaven in the parable above. Salvation is a free gift offered by Jesus, but we must give away the things that have owned us to receive what He has for us. Sometimes that means friends, family, a career, etc., but we must give what we have for the joy of stepping into His Kingdom.

Look: Stand with Jesus in this field. What does this field look like, what has been growing here? And where do you think the treasure would be?

But now, before you can dig up the treasure, you must calculate the cost:

Look from the point of view of your past: As you stand with Jesus in this field, contemplating this hidden treasure of the Kingdom, what were some of the things you needed to let go of when you first came to Jesus? Family, friends, beliefs, jobs, etc.? Pass these people and events to Jesus and watch what He does with them.

Look from the now: What are some things the Lord is asking you today to submit to Him so that you may uncover even more of His kingdom treasure? Pass these things to the Lord as well.

Q: What does the Lord want to do with them?

Gift: "Jesus, You say that if I come to You and give You my burdens, You will give me Your light yoke;18 so Lord, I have passed You all of these people, these situations, etc. Lord, if You were to give me a gift in exchange for passing all this to You, what would that gift be?"

Q: "Why that?"

Promise: "Lord as I give You my family, friends, etc., do You have a promise You wish to speak to me?"

Journal a response from the Lord.

---

18   Matt 11:28-30.

Week 4

THE QUEST!

(MATT 13:44)

We have a tradition at our house the kids love (even though they are now teenagers), where I draw out clues and scribble riddles for them to find their Easter candy. Somewhere in hiding, are big chocolate bunnies with their names on them! But, of course, I make this as complicated as possible, making the kids run hither and yon, up and down the stairs, out the door and back in again, as they try to follow my meandering list of clues, until finally they come to the treasure—and let me assure you, there is great joy!

Such treasure hunts are joy-filled, and it is to just such a joy Jesus is pointing—a joyful search, a discovery, a glorious treasure! But it is not only the searchers who enjoy the hunt, but the parents as well; just as our Father in heaven and the angels, as well, experience joy when we discover His hidden treasure.

Declaration: "Lord, we are searching for Your treasure. We have discovered some of this treasure of the Kingdom when we got saved—but there is still more! We are still learning and growing in knowing You as "Abba,"[19] in understanding the ways you speak, touch, heal, and deliver; Your kingdom is always expanding!"

Look: "Lord, let's step back into this field again; when you look at me searching for this treasure, what is the look on Your face?"

---

19   Rom 8:15, 17; Gal 4:6. Abba is an intimate term for father.

The Lord's Heart: "Lord, as I look for Your hidden treasure, what do You feel in Your heart toward me?"

Q: "Why that look, Lord; why that feeling in Your heart?"

Gift: "Lord, we know Your Word says that if our earthly fathers know how to give good gifts to their children, how much more will our heavenly Father give good gifts to His children. Lord if You could give me a gift as a clue that would help me find this treasure, what would it be?"

Q: "Why that gift, Jesus?"

Journal and dialog with the Lord about anything He showed you or told you.

Week 5

THE TREASURE!
(MATT 13:44)

There are times in our lives when we are surprised by other's kindness, by a discovery, or by a gift we didn't expect. And there is a moment in the midst of the surprise that we don't believe our eyes. We didn't see it coming! We think, "Could this really be for me?" And when we realize that yes, this is meant for us, we can't contain our joy—just as Jesus would have it when we open our heavenly treasure chest.

What God has for you!

Look: Pull that treasure chest out of the ground with Jesus. What does this treasure chest look like? How big is it? How old do you think it is?

Q: Can you open it or does Jesus have to open it for you?

Look: Ask Jesus to pass you some of the items out of the treasure chest.

Q: If there was a royal crown in that chest for you, what would it look like?

Q: What color gems would be in that crown?

Q: Ask Jesus why those colors of gems.

Q: If there was a robe (representing your royalty) in this chest for you from Jesus, what would it look like?

Q: What colors or symbols would be on that robe?

Promise: Could there be a scroll in this chest with a promise from the Father for you?

Reach into the treasure chest: does the Lord have anything else in there for you?

Q: "Lord, why that robe with those colors and symbols? Lord, why that crown? Why those colors of gems? Why that promise? Why did you place those items for me in that treasure chest?"

Journal: Spend some time with the Lord journaling out His loving response to you.

We have our treasure! But the Lord is always so giving that I would keep this treasure box and peer into it once in a while to see if anything else shows up—you never know with the Lord.

Week 6

WHAT IS TO COME

(MATT 13:44)

You now have a treasure; and a person with a treasure has a vastly different future than a person who does not. Is there any way you can find out from the Lord what will change for you now that you have this treasure of the kingdom? Yes there is! Isaiah 55:9-11 informs us that the word of God produces things just like the rain and the snow—and a crop results! The water causes grain to sprout up, grow. In just that way, when God speaks to us, things in our lives will begin to change and grow, and our gifts and abilities multiply—in other words we, too, begin to sprout! When we listen to and ponder God's word, as we have in our previous devotional activations, God's words grow in us.

Review the Promises and Treasure

In the above activations, the Lord has been speaking to you using promises, gifts as symbols, and journaling, all to convey His words of love over your life. And these words are intended to produce good things in you, to cause you to grow into His image, to become more like Jesus, and to grow in faith and confidence that His kingdom will come. This being the case, review the last three activations. Reread your journal entries, pay attention to any gifts the Lord gave you, and review what the Lord gave you in the treasure chest. When you are done, proceed to the next activation.

What is to Come

Q: "Lord, these things I have reviewed are going to produce good fruit in me. These words You have given are going to grow. Since John 16:13 tells me that the Holy Spirit will show me what is to come, would You do that please? Would You give me a foretaste of what You are going to produce in my life, with all You have spoken and given me?"

Look: Ponder those journals. Picture putting on that robe, wearing that crown, and putting your foot on that treasure chest. Then let's ask the Lord this question:

Q: "Lord, I choose to believe that I am part of the royal priesthood, and I receive these promises and treasures You have purchased for me. Jesus would You fast-forward this picture one year, two years, five years, ten years: Lord, what is going to grow, what is going to develop for me, now that I have this treasure?"

Look: After Jesus has fast-forwarded into the future the picture of you with this kingdom treasure, how have you changed and grown? Look to see.

The Lord's Heart: When the Lord looks at you in this preferable future, having watched you grow up carrying what He has given you, how does He feel? What does He see?

Promise: What promise would the Lord like to give you?

Journal and dialog with the Lord regarding anything He has shown you or told you.

(Keep in mind a day is like a thousand years to the Lord, so these time frames are symbolic; but we are given some idea what we are going to grow into!)

Week 7

THE PRODIGAL SON
(LUKE 15:11-32)

In the years I have been in ministry, I have encountered a recurring theme: the enemy attacks to deprive us of intimacy with our Father. If the enemy (or our own poor decisions) can make us look away from our Father in shame, fear, or anger, the enemy has won; our adversary's cunning scheme has been successful and we have allowed him to deprive us of connection with the God who loves us.

Fortunately, the Father has no lack of intimate love to give, and even if we turn away from Him, He never turns away from us. Case in point, the story of the prodigal son:

We catch up to the youngest son as he comes to his senses, realizes the evil he has done, and is on his way back home. The account continues:

But while he was still a long way off, his father saw him and was filled with compassion for him: he ran to his son, threw his arms around him and kissed him. (Luke 15:20)

On the Road With the Prodigal

We have all had moments in our past when we have failed the Father and realized we needed to turn around and come home: Perhaps it was the day we were saved, or when we realized we were in sin or out of God's will. In this regard, we find ourselves on the road with the prodigal son coming home to his father; for in reality, Jesus isn't just telling a story of a prodigal son: He is telling the story of a prodigal race—

81

mankind—and His heavenly Father's desire to have us back under His roof again.

Turning the Clock Back

Think back to that time when you were far from God, standing on that road like the prodigal son, and walking toward your Father's house. How far away did your Father's house feel when you realized you needed to repent, turn around, and go home? Did it feel a million miles away or close? Did you feel lost being far from home, or did you feel the longing to get home?

Journal your thoughts and feelings about these things and dialog with the Lord about them.

Looking for the Father

I know that when I have done something wrong to someone else, or I feel like I have failed the Father, sometimes the last thing I want to do is look up at Him—and that is not an uncommon problem. When I am teaching a class and people are struggling with shame or guilt, they intuitively drop their heads and stare at the floor. But there is a better posture, a New Testament posture: to stand tall and lift up our heads![20] For, as we turn toward our Father's house and look up, we realize He is running down the front steps, right toward us! Luke 15:20 informs us that the father took matters into his own hands, for, when he saw his son still far away, he took off running towards him.

Therefore, when we stand on this road of repentance, let's embrace the Father running toward us, with His forgiveness.

Look: What is the expression on the Father's face as He runs toward you?

---

20   Luke 21:28.

The Father's Heart: Ask the Father why that expression? Ask the Father what He was feeling as He ran to you?

Feel: What does it feel like to have the Father approach you at a run?

Promise: If the Lord could shout a promise to you as He runs your way, what would it be?

Journal: Record your questions and all of the Lord's loving responses as you journal.

Week 8

A MIGHTY RUN AND LOVING EMBRACE

(LUKE 15:11-32)

Have you ever experienced someone offering you grace when you didn't deserve it? I remember when I crashed my car, as a teenager, and people got hurt. I felt very guilty and full of shame; but, when my dad showed up, he put his arm around me and asked if I was ok. The accident was partially my fault: I deserved anger, but what I got was grace. And when my dad put his hand on my shoulder in love, I could feel the weight of the shame and guilt drain out of me. Warmth, surprisingly and suddenly, returned to my soul, as if the sun had just broken out from behind the clouds. Something like this may have happened to you as well, as unexpected grace came your way, possibly from a friend, a coach, a parent, or a spouse. Do you remember that moment and what it felt like for that burden to roll off your shoulders? Jesus is preparing you for that same kind of poignant moment the prodigal experienced— expecting judgment, but instead, receiving the warmth of grace.

> But while he was still a long way off, his father saw him and
> was filled with compassion for him; he ran to his son, threw
> his arms around him and kissed him. (Luke 15:20)

Look: The Father has run up to you in your last journal entry; now let Him put His arms around you; what does that look like?

Feel: What does it feel like to be hugged by Abba Father? Relax, take a deep breath, picture the scene, and allow Abba to hug and kiss you.

85

Look: Since colors in Scripture have a variety of meanings, it is possible that each kiss is imparting something different! (E.g., green for growth, purple for royalty, blue for revelation, red for the blood of Christ, etc.)

Q: As the Father is hugging you and kissing you on the cheeks, what colors in the spirit-realm are being left on your cheeks?

Q: Ask the Lord why those colors.

Promise: The Father now has you in His arms. Does He have a promise for you?

Journal and dialog with the Lord regarding everything He showed you and told you.

Week 9

THE BEST ROBE
(LUKE 15:11-32)

Have you ever won a prize, a ribbon, or a trophy? Or maybe you have received an invitation to go somewhere that felt a little out of your league, but the person bringing you thought you would be great? If so, you may have a bit of a feel for what happens next: the prodigal son feels out of his league—he is no longer worthy to be a son. In fact, becoming a hired servant, for him, would be better than he deserved. But his father isn't done lavishing love on him. And, just as it is with the prodigal son and his father, so it is with us and our heavenly Father. In fact, Abba Father is only getting started! You've won the trophy, the ribbon—it's your party and you didn't even know it! That is why the Father shouts back at the house, "Bring the best robe!" This was a robe saved for special occasions, for birthdays and feasts. And now it is yours! What have you done to deserve it? You turned around. What great joy your turning and coming to the Father has brought!

Look: Ask our Abba Father to present you with this special festival robe. What colors are on it? Are there any symbols or patterns? Is it long, is it short, is it light, is it heavy?

Q: "Why does it look like that, Father?"

Promise: Does this robe come with a promise from the Father?

Feel: What does it feel like to wear your Father's special robe?

The Father's Heart: And how does the Father feel putting it on you?

Journal the Lord's response to these questions and dialog with Him about all He showed you or told you.

Week 10

THE RING OF AUTHORITY

(LUKE 15:11-32)

As a young man, I did an embarrassing thing once: I was single and there was a very pretty young lady that worked behind the meat counter of the local grocery store. We had chatted a few times, and she had a very nice smile, so I thought I would ask her out for coffee. As I was standing in line (once again pretending to be interested in the meat on display), I looked up to see her wrapping up the purchase of the person in front of me—only to notice the ring on her finger! At that precise moment she looked up to take my order. My mouth opened and closed a few times, (my well-rehearsed speech was now highly inappropriate), and I did the only thing I could do—I bolted for the door!

A most embarrassing story, but it makes the point: the sight of a ring at the wrong moment can bring the heart to a stop, because that ring sent a message—this young lady was taken! And that is the same kind of powerful impact that the father in the parable was offering his son. This was no ordinary ring: it was a ring of authority. A signet ring! This ring would allow this lost son to once again conduct business in the name of the family. At that time, when a document was written out on a scroll and that scroll was being sealed, a blob of wax was poured on the scroll and the signet ring was pressed into that wax to show the family's crest or symbol. Thus, everyone knew the scroll was an official document from that family. Once again, this young son had his family seal. And as he walked through the town, everyone would look at his hand and see the ring; they would know this was no slave, this was no servant—this was a son with authority. Once again, the point Jesus was making is that we, too, have been taken back into the family, and not just taken back, but we have been sealed with the Holy Spirit![21] We once again carry our family's ring for the world to see.

Look: Ask the Lord about your ring. What kind of metal would it be made of? What color stones would be in that ring? Would there be any inscriptions or symbols on it?

Promise: Since all the promises of God are yes and amen in Jesus,[22] would there be a promise inscribed on that ring?

Feel: What would it feel like to wear that ring?

Journal: Ask the Lord why that ring, why that color, why that promise, why those symbols or metal? Write down what the Lord has shown you and dialog with Him about it.

---

21   Eph 1:13.
22   2 Cor 1:20.

Week 11

A NEW PAIR OF SHOES

(LUKE 15:11-32)

Imagine not being allowed to wear shoes while driving, going to work, or walking through the supermarket. Whether it is sunny or rainy, snowing or so baking hot that your feet burn on the pavement, shoes would be off limits to you. Could people really be so inhumane as to deprive someone of such a basic necessity? Yes, if you were a slave in Jesus' day, you were not allowed to wear shoes. It was a sign of shame, so that everyone could tell who and what you were. It's awfully hard to hide a pair of bare feet in a crowd. And it seems it was in just such a condition that the prodigal son was coming home to his father. Barefoot. The prodigal had been stripped down to nothing and he had walked the many miles home in his bare feet. But the father didn't see his boy's shame, he saw his calling: his sonship, his authority. He saw the treasure that his son was. Even when the son saw his shame, the father saw his destiny. This is a beautiful picture of what our heavenly Father wishes to do for us: remove our shame, cover our walk, and establish our calling and the treasure He sees us to be.

Look: If the Lord had new of shoes for you today, what kind would they be? Would they be runners or dancing shoes? Would they be army boots or slippers? And what color would they be?

Q: Ask the Lord why those kinds of shoes.

Promise: Ask the Lord to put a promise on the soles of your new shoes that would go with you everywhere you step. What promise would the Lord like to put on the soles of your new shoes?

Feel: Take some time to walk around in your new shoes. What does it feel like to wear shoes like that? Enjoy that feeling of peace or freedom, rest or joy, because that is what these shoes convey from the Father for you!

Journal: Write down anything you see, hear, feel, etc., and then allow the Lord to respond as you write.

LIVING IN OUR ENSEMBLE

(LUKE 15:11-32)

Think of a time when you were dressed up and everyone was waiting to look at you. You walked out in your very best ensemble to waiting admirers. How did that feel? All eyes were upon you—and you looked good! In our culture, the closest thing with which we can compare what the prodigal is experiencing is a wedding when the doors open and the bride walks in. We can't wait to look at the bride whom we love, in her beautiful dress. For men in our culture, making that sports team and walking out among the fans for the first time, or going to our wedding or graduation, may possibly be the equivalent. It is at just such a moment when we meet up with our prodigal one more time—expecting judgement and loss, but instead, receiving grace and blessing—indeed, being celebrated as the guest of honor!

Q: Now that the Lord has you dressed as He wants you to be, wearing this symbolic robe of honor, this ring of authority, these shoes of freedom, and He can eye you up and down, what would He want to say to you?

Look: Since 1 Corinthians 2:16 says you have the mind of Christ, invite Jesus into this scene where you are standing before the Father, wearing your ring, robe, and shoes. Notice where Jesus would stand, sit or lean.

Ask Jesus to allow you to stand in His shoes and look through His eyes. When Jesus sees you wearing this robe, ring, and shoes from the Father, what does He see? How does He feel? Do you look like a servant or a son? What kind of authority does He see on you? What is the expression on Jesus' face when He looks at you?

Future View: Since John 16:13 tells us the Holy Spirit can show us what is to come, ask Jesus about it: "Lord, if I receive these gifts from the Father and I keep them on and I choose to believe I have been given the choice robe, the ring of authority, and shoes of freedom, what is going to change for me? Where do I go from here? How am I going to grow and move forward?"

With these questions in mind, ask the Lord to fast-forward this picture of you wearing this robe, ring, and shoes into the future. If you receive and wear these things, how is life going to change for you in five years, in ten years?

Journal: Watch for changes, record all you see, sense, and feel, and dialog with the Lord about it.

Community Application: As you continue to wear this robe, ring, and shoes, you are going to produce fruit that you will be able to give away to others. That being the case, ask the Lord how growing in the authority of the ring, robe, and shoes that He has given will result in you influencing those around you in your church, community, and the world.

Promise: "Lord do You have a promise for me, as well?"

Journal what you have seen, your questions for the Lord, and allow the Lord to respond and reveal His heart to you!

Week 13

Walking in the Anointing

(Luke 15:11-32)

Now, after all you have done, you want to learn to walk in what God has given you. When God gives us something, it carries an anointing, and the word *anointing* means to "rub on." The question then is, what does the Lord want to anoint you with, or "rub on you" by wearing this ring, this robe, and these shoes? You can find out by being aware of what you sense in your spirit while you interact with these items from the Lord. When you do this, He gives you an aspect of anointing from what these symbolic items carry: peace, joy, power, healing, holiness, rest, etc. You don't want to treat the things God gives you as just mental images to interpret, but as impartations from your Father, designed as resources from Him for your daily life.

Step into what God has for you!

To do this activation properly will require some space. Find a place where you can walk ten to twenty feet forwards and back. You want to activate your faith just as the Lord did by having the children of Israel march around Jericho,[23] and having Naaman bathe seven times in the Jordan,[24] as well as Jesus, Himself, telling the blind man to bathe in the pool of Siloam.[25] Sometimes a little bit of movement can get us out of our heads and into our hearts.

---

23   Josh 6:4-5.
24   2 Kings 5:10.
25   John 9:7.

Following the Prodigal

In the parable, the prodigal son did a lot of walking. He first walked away from his father and what the ring, robe, and shoes represented. Then, when he came to his senses, he walked back home and received from his father what these gifts imparted. To help us learn to be aware of the "anointing" in the robe, ring, and shoes that our heavenly Father has given us, we, too, are going to walk the prodigal's walk and see how that would feel.

1. Ask Jesus to come and stand with you in the place you have chosen.

2. Now, picture your robe, and ask Jesus to place it about 10 to 20 feet away.

3. While you are standing with Jesus, across the room from your robe, turn your back on the robe and face the other direction. How does that feel? Pay attention to what you sense in your spirit.

If that robe is just a picture, that is fine—you may sense nothing; but there may be more from the Lord then just the picture of the robe. If you don't feel anything, look at the picture. Did the picture change? You will also want to pay attention to what the Spirit is revealing to you about your robe by sensing what it contains from the Lord. If you feel you are losing something by turning your back on your robe, you are actually "discerning" with your spirit what God has placed in that robe: an anointing—for you!

4. To make this sensing activation stronger, try to take a step away from the robe. (You might not be able to do this; people who are very spiritually sensitive may be sensing/feeling enough already). Can you do it? How much of an effort was trying to take a step away from your robe? (Trying to step away is one way to find out what anointing the robe contains from the Lord and what you

would lose by not accepting it. This increases the value of what the robe means to you.)

Those of you who are spiritually sensitive may have been significantly impacted by trying to walk away.26 Others may have felt it to some degree, or pictured it. No matter, it is good to learn to be aware of what is going on in your spirit. And what you have discerned in turning your back gives you some clues as to what that robe contains from God for you—what its value truly is. That is what you need to discover—what you lose from the Lord if you don't put this robe on.

Turning Back

1. Now turn around and face the robe.

2. Slowly walk over to the robe, while being aware of what you are sensing and picturing.

Look: What do you see when you approach the robe? What is happening with the robe?

Feel: What does it feel like to approach the robe? Contrast that to what it felt like to walk away from the robe: What is the difference between the two actions? Where are you experiencing that feeling in your being?

Look: Let the Lord put the robe on you. What do you see?

Feel: How does it feel for the Lord to put the robe on you?

Promise: Does the Lord want to give you a promise as you wear His robe?

---

26   If so, my book *Keepers of the Presence* may be a good resource for you.

Journal the above experience and write down what the Lord has to say to you about accepting His robe.

Walking Away From and Toward the Ring

Follow the steps laid out for the robe above, but this time, with the ring.

Walking Away From and Toward the Shoes

Follow the steps laid out above, but this time, with the shoes.

Week 14

A NEW NAME

(LUKE 15:11-32)

Names are powerful things. There is the name our parents have given us, but also names we call ourselves, and names other people call us—some of which are not so nice: "Loser," "Dummy," etc. You get the idea. Fortunately for us, God also has names He likes to call us: "Beloved," "Faithful One," "Overcomer," etc.27

Take some time to put on the ring, robe, and shoes again, then stand before your Father and get Him to pronounce over you the names He would like you to be called.

Look: Look at the Father's face. What expression does He have, as you approach Him for this blessing?

Now ask the Father,

Q: "Abba Father what name would You like to pronounce over me as I wear Your ring?"

Q: "Abba Father what name would You like to pronounce over me as I wear Your robe?"

Q: "Abba Father what name would You like to pronounce over me as I wear Your shoes?"

---

27   Isa 62.

99

Journal the Lord's responses to these questions. Allow the Lord to tell you why He would choose these names for you. Finish by thanking the Lord for all He has shown you and done for you through this set of activations.

Week 15

THE GOOD SAMARITAN

(LUKE 10:30-37)

Have you ever been knocked down hard—and then surprised by who helped you up? Many years ago, I went through burn out. I lost my ministry, a lot of friends, hope, and my ability to love. In the process, I discovered some interesting and surprising things about people: some of the people I thought would help didn't, and those that I thought wouldn't, did. And in the end, God taught me more than I could have ever imagined about His compassion, care, and grace.

Pondering the above makes me think of the story of the Good Samaritan. Those who should have helped the beaten man, such as the priest and Levite, passed him by. And the one who did help him—the Good Samaritan—didn't have to. How about you? Have you ever been in need of help? And were you surprised by whom the Lord sent?

A Fresh Look at the Good Samaritan

Invite the Lord to step with you into the story of the Good Samaritan and stand with Him. Look at this poor fellow who is waylaid along the road.

Look: Where would Jesus stand, sit, or kneel?

Look: What is the expression on Jesus' face as He gazes upon this unfortunate traveller?

Along comes the Samaritan

Look: What is the expression on Jesus' face toward the Samaritan as he approaches this poor traveller?

Look: Ask Jesus to allow you to step into His shoes and look through His eyes.

Q: What does Jesus see and feel towards this Samaritan and the good he is doing?

Q: What would Jesus like to say to the Good Samaritan?

Gift: If Jesus could give the Samaritan a gift, what would it be?

Journal the Lord's response and dialog with Him about what He has told you and showed you.

Applying the Story to Your Life

Was there ever a time when you were left beat up on the road of life (e.g., a difficult marriage, a time of illness, a season of unemployment, troubles at work or at church, etc.)? What would it look like for you to be the one lying on the road of life, all beat up from what you had been through? Let's find out what Jesus will do for you, and then whom He will send to you.

Looking For Jesus

Look: Ask Jesus to come and meet you on your road of life, when you were beat up.

Look: As Jesus looks at you in the condition you were in, what is the expression on His face?

Q: "Why that expression, Lord?"

Promise: Does Jesus have a promise for you?

Journal what the Lord would like to say to you.

Your Good Samaritan(s)

As a traveller, beat up on the road of life, it is more than likely that a few of the people you thought would stop and help you didn't. But whom did the Lord send your way? Was it one person or many? Who were your Good Samaritan(s)? What did they do for you? And how did that help you?

Look: Step into Jesus' shoes again, look through Jesus' eyes, and feel what He feels. When Jesus looks at this person(s) helping you, what does He see; what does He feel?

Gift: If Jesus were to give this Good Samaritan a gift for helping you, what would it be? Why?

Promise: If Jesus could give the Good Samaritan a promise for helping you, what would it be?

Journal the Lord's responses and ask Him any questions you may have.

Recommendation: I would suggest to you that, if you know your Good Samaritan (or Samaritans), write them a thank-you letter, or pray blessing upon their lives today.

Week 16

BEING THE GOOD SAMARITAN

(LUKE 10:30-37)

I remember the story of a pastor who dressed up as a hobo and sat himself by the church's front door. He must have had a great disguise, because not one congregant stopped to enquire on the way into the church, as to whether he needed help.

With dramatic effect, the pastor/hobo hobbled into the service late, then proceeded to walk up the center aisle (to the chagrin, I believe, of the congregants), stand at the pulpit, and slowly remove his disguise. As the congregation finally realized who the smelly bum actually was, the shock that they didn't help him set in. The pastor calmly said, "I would like you all to read the story of the Good Samaritan. See you next week."

I am sure that we have all placed ourselves firmly in that congregation, feeling what it would be like to be the one who walked past. But the on the other hand: there have been times when you have stopped and helped. It may have been a stranger; it may have been someone you've known. It may be that if you didn't help this person, no one else would have. It could have been a spouse, a friend, a parent, a child, someone visiting the church, or someone whom you have never met before. But at some point in time *you* were the Good Samaritan. I wonder how that made Jesus feel? Let's find out.

The Samaritan Who Helped

Q: If you think about your life and all of the people whom you have helped through the years, whom would Jesus bring to mind?

Look: What would be the condition of this person (or business, or ministry, etc.) lying on the road of life? Look to see.

Look: As you stop to help this person, what is the look on Jesus' face?

Promise: Does the Lord have a promise for you, now that you have helped this person?

Gift: Does Jesus have a gift He would like to give you, now that you have helped this person?

Journal anything the Lord showed you or said to you, and dialog with Him about it.

Living in the Present

Now, step into the present moment and step back onto the Samaritan's road one more time, with Jesus.

Look: As you walk with Jesus today, who do you see lying on the road of life right now?

Q: What would the Lord like you to do for them?

Journal the Lord's response, and ask Him any questions you have.

Week 17

MARY AND MARTHA

(LUKE 10:38-42)

Have you ever been invited to a party with a group of friends? Possibly a party held in your honor?

Picture this: the hostess (or host) has opened up her house to you. But her helper is too busy wanting to be with you than do the preparations for which she is responsible. The hostess approaches you quietly on the side and asks you if you would help motivate her set-up person to "get to it." Your response? You tell her that her set-up person is too busy listening to you right now!

These kinds of "get the party started" dynamics are common but not new. In fact, we find these dynamics going on at Martha's house the day Jesus and His disciples stopped by.

Get the Party Started

Jesus and His disciples had just come into town and Martha had been kind enough to open up her house to them. But Martha's help, her sister Mary, was sitting at Jesus' feet instead of helping Martha get the party started. Martha was doing all the work while her partner had abandoned her! I have often wondered if Jesus felt pressured to smile and agree with Martha that Mary needed to help too. After all, it was Martha's house, she was the one who invited Jesus and the disciples in, and she was the one who ended up doing all of the work. What could have motivated Jesus to respond to Martha the way He did? Let's step into the story and find out.

Mary Sitting at Jesus Feet

As we step into the room, we find Mary sitting at Jesus' feet. There is Martha, looking at Mary. And as we look at Martha, let's examine her statements to Jesus about Mary:

> Lord don't you care [expressing doubt]
>
> that my sister has left me [expressing abandonment]
>
> to do the work by myself? [expressing isolation]
>
> Tell her to help me! [expressing exasperation][28]

Look: What is the expression on Martha's face as she is looking at Mary?

Look: What is the expression on Martha's face as she looks at Jesus?

Mary's Point of View

Look: Picture Mary, sitting at Jesus' feet as He teaches.

Look: What is the look on Mary's face as she has forgotten about everything else except Jesus?

Journal: Ask the Lord why Mary is looking at Him like that.

Q: Ask the Lord if that look is important. If so, why?

---

28   Luke 10:41. It may be important to note that Jesus does not correct Martha for working; He corrects her for worrying.

You've Got the Look

People's expressions can tell us a lot about what they are thinking, as an expression is an extension of the heart. When we are exasperated, our shoulders are tense, our arms are crossed, our eyebrows are up, our lips are pursed, and our eyes may be shooting daggers. When we are looking at the one we love, likely our shoulders are relaxed, our posture open, our eyes peacefully focused, and our mouth carrying the curve of a smile. These are two very different ways to show up. Mary had chosen one, Martha another. An *expression* reveals an *emotion,* which reveals what we are *thinking.*

Putting on the Right Look

Look: Let's step into the scene with Mary again and look at her looking at Jesus.

Look: What is the expression on her face?

Look: What is her posture like?

Q: What do you think she is feeling as she looks at the Lord like that?

Q: And what does that tell you Mary believes about Jesus?

Journal what you see, sense, or anything the Lord said to you, and dialog with Jesus about it.

Stepping Into Mary's Shoes

Have you ever looked at Jesus the way Mary is looking at Jesus?

Look: Take some time and sit down with Mary (sit just like her) and look at Jesus just the way she does.

Feel: How does that feel?

Q: Looking at Jesus with that expression, feeling those feelings, what would you like to say to Jesus?

Gift: If the Lord could give you a gift for sitting and listening to Him like Mary, what would it be?

Q: Why that?

Journal your experience and what Jesus would like to say in response.

Watching for Inner Growth

Sitting like Mary, feeling like Mary, and believing like Mary yield powerful results. We become different people—loving and focused people—if we imitate Mary.

Look: "Lord, if I learn to gaze at You like Mary did, what doors will open for me?"

Look: "Where could You take me and meet with me that You couldn't otherwise?"

Look: "What will be a secret place that will be made available to me if I learn to look at You like Mary did?"

Q: "Why there?"

Q: "What would You like to do together there, Lord?"

Gift: "And Lord, if I learn to meet You there, would you have a gift for me?"

Journal what the Lord has shown you and anything He would like to say to you.

Week 18

BREATH

(JOHN 20:22)

I have noticed that, once in a while, on a warm summer's day, there is a poignant fragrance from the pine trees floating down from the mountains some distance away, mixed with this incredible, fresh warm breeze that blows in from the interior of the province. And when it happens, I stop, turn my face to the Lord and say, "Thank you," because at that moment I am reminded of the joys of being filled with the Holy Spirit.

Breath = Wind = Spirit

In Scripture, the words translated for "wind," "breath," and "the Spirit" are the Hebrew word *ruwach* and the Greek word *pneuma*. This is why Jesus "breathed" on His disciples in John 20:22 and said to them, *"Receive the Holy Spirit."* This same symbolic connection between "wind" and the "Holy Spirit" continues in Acts 2:2, when the disciples, waiting in the upper room, were suddenly filled with the Holy Spirit while encountering the blowing of a mighty wind.

We, too, are to encounter this same breath, wind, Holy Spirit. So, if Jesus was to breathe His breath on you—the wind of the Holy Spirit—what would it look like? What would it sound like? What fragrance from heaven would be carried on that Holy Wind?

113

Let the Wind Blow

Begin by having a talk with Jesus: a back and forth conversation based on relationship (*koinonia*) with Him. Let's begin by talking with Him about a meeting place.

Look: If you could pick a place to meet Jesus today, where would you pick? What would be the perfect place?

Q: Why that place? Tell Jesus why that would be the perfect place today.

Look: "Lord, You know the place I would pick to meet You. Jesus, if You could pick a place to meet me today where would You pick?"

Q: "And why would You pick that place?"

Journal what the Lord tells you and talk with Him about it.

The Wind and the Spirit

Q: "Lord, we know from Scripture that the word for "wind," "breath," and "spirit," is the same word, and that the wind is a symbol for receiving the Holy Spirit. So Lord, I ask You to breathe upon me today!"

Look: Meeting the Lord in this place, watch as He breathes upon you.

Q: If the Lord's breath had a color that enveloped you as He breathed upon you, what would that color be today?

Q: Ask the Lord why that color?

Listen: "Lord, if Your breath had a sound as You breathed on me, what would it be?"

Q: "Lord, Scripture talks about the 'fragrance' of Christ. If Your breath—this wind that You blow upon me—had a fragrance, what would it be?"[29]

Feel: How does the whole experience make you feel? What fruit of the Holy Spirit are you experiencing as you interact with Jesus and He breathes on you?[30]

Journal what the Lord reveals to you about the color, sound, and fragrance of His wind/breath, keeping in mind that we are working with the symbol of the Holy Spirit. Ask the Lord why that color, sound, fragrance, and that fruit of the Holy Spirit; unpack it all as you and the Lord talk as friends.

---

29   2 Cor 2:15.
30   Gal 5:22.

Week 19

PONDERING THE WIND OF THE SPIRIT

(ACTS 2:2)

After Jesus breathed on His disciples, and the wind of the Spirit blew upon them, things changed.[31] They got bold! And it really unnerved the Pharisees; they realized these untrained men had been with Jesus.[32] Just as it was with the disciples, when Jesus fills us with His Spirit, things begin to change for us. We become more and more like Jesus—peaceful, caring, loving, bold, understanding, etc.—and we can observe that change in ourselves as we walk with Jesus.[33]

Ponder: Think about last week's devotional. Meet with Jesus once again in that meeting place, and ponder the color of His breath upon you, the sounds you heard, the fragrance you smelled, and the fruit of the Holy Spirit you experienced.

As you ponder all of those aspects of God's breath, consider how the continual power and influence of God's breath upon you will maintain a process of transformation in you, to the end that you will continually grow into the polished gem He envisioned as your destiny.

---

31   Acts 2:22.
32   Acts 4:13.
33   2 Cor 3:17-18.

As Time Goes By: Watching for the Effect

Q: "Lord we are to be filled continually with the Holy Spirit.[34] So, if I let You keep breathing upon me time and time again, month after month, year after year, allowing the wind of the Holy Spirit to fill me up, what is going to change in my life as time goes by? What is going to be the effect?"

Look: Stand with the Lord, and let Him keep breathing upon you.

Q: What happens after each breath? What changes? For example, do you grow taller? Do you become more peaceful, radiant, joyful, etc.? What happens around you? Do flowers grow? Does the sun come out from behind the clouds, etc.?

Q: How does each breath of the Spirit affect you?

Q: What color is the first breath?

Look: Now, watch for the effect of the breath upon you. What grows, what changes?

Q: What about the second breath? Watch for the effect.

Q: What about the third? The fourth? The fifth? The sixth?

Listen: What sound did you hear with the first breath?

Look: And now, watch for the effect of that sound upon you. What grows? What changes?

Listen: What was the second sound? It's effect?

---

34   Acts 2:4-8; 6:8; Eph 5:18.

Listen: The third? The fourth? The fifth? The sixth?

Q: What fragrance did you smell with the first breath?

Look: Now, watch for the effect of that fragrance upon you. What grows? What changes?

Q: What was the effect of the second fragrance?

Q: The third? The fourth? The fifth? The sixth?

Journal what the Lord tells you about each breath, sound, and fragrance.

Journal the effects and the changes you experience after each. Discuss with the Lord why He is changing you in that way, and what promises He would like to speak over your life in the process.

Week 20

THE BIRD

(MATT 6:26)

One glorious fall day, while dealing with some fears and concerns about God providing for me and my family, I decided to go out for a walk in the woods.

As I pondered life and listened to the leaves crunching under my shoes, I came around a corner and discovered an unexpected treasure: a hidden wooden walkway over a reed covered marsh. This mysterious walkway curled its way through the water and reeds, which were hiding fish, turtles, and frogs. Caught up in exploring my little discovery, I soon realized I had taken up too much time, gone too far, gotten lost, and needed to turn around.

My little discovery was beautiful indeed, but the walkway was a little thin in places and, up ahead, blocking my way across, was a young man with a stroller, bending over his son. It was a bit annoying at first, because I couldn't get past them to be on my way. So I pretended to look at the long grass, the frogs, and the like.

I watched as the young father stood up holding a small see-through bag of seeds. He opened the bag and poured some of the contents out into his open hand and held it out. To my surprise, this was a signal to the creatures of the woodland to spring into action. A squirrel hopped out of the woods from up the path and hurried down the walkway for the free food offering. Chickadees also began to make their appearance in the bushes around the man, the stroller, and his young son.

"Watch, Conner, watch!" The young father said to his son. Conner, being pretty young, appeared not to notice that the squirrel and birds were very close; he looked at whatever caught his attention. And then, my attention was caught: one of the chickadees flew out of the bushes and landed on the man's open hand. He hopped around the hand, enjoying the savories saved up for him. Conner took great delight in this. It was a marvelous spectacle indeed—this small bird being fed in the hands of his father.

The Goodness of the Father

There are parables from Jesus everywhere for us to see—if we can learn to slow down and look. I had almost missed one such parable, with hungry creatures of the woodland, and a father with his small son, set out intentionally in front of me. I was in such a hurry to figure out where I was and get to where I needed to be, that I wasn't looking for God. All the while a living story was out right in front of me, containing exactly what I needed to hear from the Father:

> Look at the birds of the air; they do not sow or reap or store away in barns, and yet your heavenly Father feeds them. Are you not much more valuable than they? (Matt 6:26, NIV)

This was the very issue I had been concerned about on my walk in the woods that day—God's provision. And if I hadn't been blocked on the walkway, I would not have seen what the Lord wanted to show me.

Slowing Down to Look

God wants to show us how He takes care of those around us, just as this father was demonstrating to his young son. So take a moment, slow down, and see what the Father is doing around you. Ask the Father to show you how He is bending down to open His hand to three of His children you know:

- a close friend

- a parent or a child

- a minister

Setting up a Meeting Place

Look: Ask Jesus where He would like to meet you today (or pick a favorite place where you would like to meet Jesus).

Q: Ask Jesus where He would like to stand, sit, or kneel in this meeting place.

Look: As we watched the little bird fly to the father's hand in the story above, do the same thing here. Watch how the Lord takes care of one of your friends whom you have invited into this meeting place picture.

Gift: "Lord, since every good and perfect gift comes down from the Father, I know you have a great gift for my friend. If you have a gift for my friend today, what is it?"

Q: "Why that?"

Promise: "Lord, we know that all the promises are "yes" in Christ Jesus.35 So, if you were to give my friend a promise today, Lord what would it be?"

Q: "Why that?"

Repeat the process with both a parent or a child, and a minister you appreciate.

---

35   2 Cor 1:20.

Journal what the Lord shows you, and ask the Lord questions about the revelation He has given you.

Week 21

WATCHING THE FATHER

(JOHN 20:22)

Jesus said He only did what He saw His Father doing. This is a great time to have that same experience. We have watched as Jesus gave your friend, parent/child, and minister a gift, and a promise. But we can do more than that: we can also feel the joy God experiences in His giving of the gift and promise as well. We can begin to do this by learning to observe the expression on Jesus' face as we watch Him interact with those we love. As expressions can be intricate and delicate, they often inspire a whole variety of discussions between us and the Lord. These expressions cause us to connect with exactly what the Lord wants us to connect with—His heart—as expressions of His face are always connected to what is occurring in His heart.

Look: What is the expression on the Lord's face as He gives your friend, minister, and parent or child this gift and promise? (You may see it, sense it, or "know it in your knower.")

Q: "Jesus, why did You have that expression as You interacted with my friend, parent or child, or minister?"

Journal what you saw, sensed, what the Lord said, etc., and any questions you may have for the Lord.

Repeat this process for your parent or child, minister.

Week 22

SEEING THROUGH JESUS' EYES

(1 COR 2:16)

Mind of Christ

Go back to your meeting place from last week and watch again as the Lord gives your friend, parent or child, and minister a gift and a promise.

Now add another step: looking at the event through Jesus' eyes.

Look: First Corinthians 2:16 says we have the mind of Christ, so step into the Lord's shoes and look through His eyes at your friend to see what Jesus sees and feel what He feels. We are going to do this by stepping right into Jesus in the picture and looking from His perspective. Now, let's discuss all of this with the Lord.

Look: Look around the picture Jesus has given you of a meeting place with Him and your friend. Where would Jesus be sitting, standing, etc.?

Look: Step into the Lord's shoes and look at your friend from His perspective.

The Lord's Heart: How does Jesus feel when He looks at your friend?

Q: What does Jesus see that you don't see?

Look: "Let me look through Your eyes, Jesus, as You give my friend this gift."

Q: "As my friend receives this gift, what is going to change for them from Your point of view, Jesus?"

The Lord's Heart: "What do you, feel Jesus, as You give my friend this gift?"

Promise: "As You speak this promise over my friend's life, what is going to change? From your point of view, Jesus, what do You see happening?"

Journal any revelation the Lord gave you and ask the Lord why He saw and felt that way toward your friend.

Repeat the process for both a parent/child and a minister. As well, you may want to consider giving your parent, close friend, or minister, a card of appreciation, along with a note about what the Lord has shown you. You don't need to be preachy: you could put the revelation in your own words, expressing your love and your sense of God's love for each one.

Week 23

WINGS TO FLY

You will find in Scripture that being in the air is a symbol of being "in the Spirit." In one awkward example, we find Ezekiel lifted up by his hair between heaven and earth, in front of the elders of Israel.[36] A better known example would be Isaiah 40:31, where we are told by Isaiah that those who wait upon the Lord will rise up on wings as eagles. In fact, there are many examples of being in the Spirit using different kinds of wings: eagles' wings,[37] women with storks' wings,[38] the wings of doves,[39] angels' wings, and, of course, Jesus rising up "into the clouds" without any wings at all.[40] And let's not forget John seeing an open door in the heavens and being told, "Come up here!"[41]

Since we are told in Colossians 3:1-2 that we are to set our "minds on things above and not on things below," this begs the question: How are we going to get up there? How about a symbolic pair of wings?

If the Lord could give you a set of wings today that would represent you being in the Spirit, what kind of wings would He give you? Would it be large eagles wings, butterfly wings, hummingbird wings, a superhero cape, or something else?

Look to see what kind of wings Jesus would give you.

Q: Ask Jesus why those particular wings for today.

---

36   Ezek 8:3.
37   Isa 40:31.
38   Zech 5:9.
39   Isa 55:6.
40   Acts 1:9.
41   Rev 4:1.

Q: "Lord, what colors would You like to put on these wings?"

Q: "Why those colors, Jesus?"

Promise: "How about a promise, Lord? If You were to write a promise on my wings, what would it be?"

Journal what the Lord showed and spoke to you and talk about it with Him.

LEARNING TO FLY!

Now what is the point of wings if we are not going to use them? So let's ask Jesus to take you flying. Look with the eyes of your heart to see. You may picture a place, sense it, or the Lord may tell you where it is. All are good.

Feel: How does it feel to fly with Jesus?

Look: When Jesus looks at you flying, what is the expression on His face?

Q: "Why that?"

The Lord's Heart: When the Lord looks at you flying with your wings/superhero cape, what does He see and feel from His point of view?"

Q: "Lord, if I receive these wings from You, where would You like to take me flying, and what would You like to show me today?"

Look to see where the Lord would take you flying.

Q: "Why here, Lord?"

Q: "What would You like to do together here, Jesus?"

Gift: "Lord, do You have a gift for me here? Why that?"

Journal anything the Lord shows you or tells you, and dialog with Him about it as you write.

Week 25

GETTING USED TO THE "FEEL" OF YOUR WINGS

The symbol of wings is very important for us, as wings represent our ability to connect with the Lord through the Holy Spirit. Wings (or a superhero's cape, etc.) are great symbols of being able to put our minds on things above and not things below.[42] Wings can be full of an anointing from the Lord, given so that we may be able to see and grasp what Jesus wants to reveal to us. With that in mind, today we want to work on sensing/feeling what these wings "contain" from the Lord.

Unpacking Your Wings

Go back and reread last week's journal regarding your wings. Get a picture and a sense of them—what they look and feel like—and give thanks to Jesus for them.

You are now going to discover the significance of your wings, gifted to you by Jesus. In other words, what anointing they carry. This anointing could be the fruit of the Spirit (love, peace, joy, etc.) or it could be a gift of the Spirit (healing, prophecy, power, etc.). Below is a great way to find out:

1. Ask Jesus to come and stand with you in your room or space.

2. Now, picturing those wings, ask Jesus to place them about 10 to 20 feet away.

---

42   Col 3:2.

3. While you are standing with Jesus, across the room from your wings, turn your back on the wings and face the other direction. What does that feel like? Pay attention to what you sense in your spirit.

If those wings are only a picture that is fine. You may sense nothing, but there may be more from the Lord than the picture of the wings. You will also want to pay attention to what the Spirit is revealing to you about your wings by sensing what they "contain" from the Lord. If you feel as if you may be losing something by turning your back on your wings, you are actually "discerning" with your spirit that God has placed an anointing for you in those wings!

4. To make this sensing activation stronger, try to take a step away from the wings. (You may not be able to do this—people who are very spiritually sensitive will be sensing/feeling enough already.) Can you do it? How much effort did it take to take a step away from your wings? (Trying to step away is one way to find out which anointing the wings contain from the Lord, and what you would lose by not accepting them. This increases the value of what the wings mean to you).

Journal: What do you feel you would lose or miss out on if you turned your back on this gift of wings from Jesus and walked away? Dialog with Jesus about how it would feel and why. That dialog will help you discover why you value those wings so much.43

Turning Towards

1. Now take a moment and turn toward your wings. What changes? How does it feel to turn toward your wings? It is important to learn to be aware of what you are sensing/feeling in your spirit.

---

43   It is possible that sometimes you could walk away from your wings and feel totally fine about it; as strange as that may seem. When that happens, usually the Lord wants to talk to you about making good personal choices.

2. Walk toward your wings. What does it feel like as you approach them?

What would it feel like to put those wings on?

Promise: "Jesus, do You have a promise for me if I accept and wear these wings?"

Look: Notice the look on Jesus' face as you put the wings on. What expression does He have?

Q: "Lord, why do You have that expression when I wear these wings?"

Journal everything that you felt in your spirit, or that the Lord has shown you, and discuss this experience with Jesus.

Week 26

THE BOAT
(MATT 8:23-27)

"Don't rock the boat!" is an expression people like to use when things in life are unsettled and they are afraid their troubling life situations could get even worse. No one wants to be in a boat being rocked back and forth; a "boat" being an effective symbol of our lives when day-to-day circumstances are rough. People also like to compare their lives to boats when things are "smooth sailing" and everything is going wonderfully. Therefore, boats can be a great symbol for Jesus to use in teaching us how to face the storms in our lives. When the disciples were in the boat with Jesus, they called on Him to calm the storm.[44] And, just as Jesus was with the disciples on their boat, He wants to be with us in the midst of our "life storms," on our "life boats."

What Floats Your Boat?

Q: If your life were a boat right now, what kind of boat would it be? A sail boat: are you just trusting the Lord, allowing the breath of the Holy Spirit to push you along? How about a powerboat: is there lots of activity; is your life just racing along? Possibly a paddleboat: is it just you working away at something in life by yourself, applying as much effort as you can?

With these examples in mind, what kind of boat do you find yourself in?

Journal your ponderings.

---

44   Matt 8:23-27.

The Water and Waves

We now have our boat, but how about the sea? As we mentioned earlier, sometimes life is smooth sailing and at other times we are yelling, "Don't rock the boat!" Life may seem troubled and we may be tossed back and forth by health, family, work, and other difficult situations.

Look: How is the sea of your life doing? How does the water look today? Is it calm and peaceful, or is the water unsettled, with waves moving back and forth over the surface of the sea? Take a look over the side of your boat and keep a weather eye open.

Journal what the water looks like today and what you think this may symbolize in your life.

Meeting With Jesus

Since Jesus promised to never leave you or forsake you, let's invite Him to come aboard.

Look: If Jesus could sit, stand, or lean anywhere, where would He be?

Q: "Jesus, why there?"

Journal His response.

Looking From Jesus' Point of View

Q: "Lord, when I look at the sea from my point of view, if life is going well, it may look calm and colorful, and if life is difficult, it may look stirred up and dark."

"But Lord, I know that my perspective on things and Your perspective may not be the same. Lord, can I step into Your shoes, look through Your eyes, and view the sea of my life from Your point of view?"

Look: Step right into Jesus, look through His eyes. When He looks at this sea of your life, what does He see? What does He feel?

Gift: Ask Jesus if He has a gift He would like to give you as He looks at the sea of your life.

Q: "Why that gift, Lord?"

Promise: Ask Jesus if He has as promise for you as He looks over the side of your boat.

Journal what the Lord has shown you and ask Him any questions you may have concerning why He may see the sea the same way or differently from you.

Week 27

WALKING, COMMANDING, ENJOYING, & RESTING

As we take a cursory overview of the times Jesus met with His disciples in the boat, four very different scenes come to mind:

First: Jesus commanding the wind and the waves to be still.[45]

Second: Instead of commanding the storm to ease, Jesus asking Peter to take a step of faith, get out of the boat, and walk on the water to Him.[46]

Third: Watching Jesus, who is untroubled by what the wind and waves are doing, sleeping through the storm.[47]

Fourth: Jesus preaching from the boat and asking the disciples to haul in a huge net full of fish—a great symbol of harvest and growth.[48]

Doing What You See Jesus Doing

As you observe the sea of your life with Jesus, ask Jesus what He would like to do.

---

45   Mark 6:47-51.
46   Matt 14:22-33.
47   Matt 8:23-27.
48   Luke 5:1-11.

141

Q: "Jesus, what do You want to do in this situation, with the sea looking the way it does?"

"Do You want to calm the water?"

"Do You want to take a rest?"

"Do You want to step out of the boat?"

"Jesus, do You want to show me where all the fish are?"

Look: Give Jesus permission to do what He wants to do, and watch what He does.

Q: "Jesus, why did You do that?"

Q: "Jesus, what do You want me to do in this situation?"

Gift: "Jesus, if I do what You are asking of me, do You have a gift for me?"

Promise: "Jesus, if I do what You ask of me, do You have a promise for me?"

Journal and dialog with the Lord about anything He has shown you and told you.

Week 28

LEARNING THE
LESSONS OF THE SEA

(MATT 8:23-25)

As you can imagine, the answers the Lord gave you last week will be based on your individual circumstances and what Jesus is teaching you in this season of your life. We have all had seasons, however, where Jesus has calmed a storm for us, asked us to walk on the water with Him, taught us how to catch fish, or to rest with Him in the boat and ignore the waves. As all of these different life lessons are precious treasures from the Lord, look back at past storms in your life when Jesus was teaching you these various lessons of the sea, and consider what He was imparting to you at that time.

A Time of Rest in the Boat

Q: When was there a time in your life that Jesus had you rest with Him in the midst of a storm, when your world was rocked and Jesus whispered, "Trust Me," "Be still," or, "Come to the secret place"?

Journal: Spend some time pondering what life was like back then; journal some memories, feelings, and experiences you had at that time.

Look: Peer over the side of the boat and see what the storm was like at that time in your life.

Look: Where would Jesus like to rest in the boat as that storm in your life was raging? Go and be with Jesus. Rest with Him.

Q: "Lord, during this storm in my life, why are we resting? Why not command the water to be still? Why did You want to teach me rest?"

Journal the Lord's response, any questions you may have, and the Lord's answers.

Q: "Lord, as I am at rest with You here in this boat, learning to be still and know You are God—what is happening with the storm outside?"

Q: "Lord, as I was learning to rest with You in this "life storm," how did this change my life?

Gift: "Lord, as I rest with You, do You have a gift for me?"

Q: "Why that gift, Lord?"

Promise: "Lord, as I rest with You, do you have a promise?"

Journal the Lord's response, any questions you may have, and His answers.

Moving On

It is time to add a new listening to Jesus skill in an activation I like to call, "Moving On." This activation is based on our earlier work, "setting + thought + feeling = action." This strategic exercise will occur a few times over the next few journal entries.

As you have been in the boat, sitting with Jesus, you have been working through some stressful life situations in which Jesus has taught you how to apply rest and peace principles. He reviewed with you the thoughts, feelings, and actions that you experienced in these trials. Now you have grasped these life lessons; you've "moved on" in your spiritual development; in essence, you have graduated. Your thoughts, feelings, and responses are different. For example, you may be more at rest under stress, you may be able to trust the Lord more easily and to minister peace to others from what you have received from Him. Learning these life lessons and maturing—in this case, in the area of rest and peace—enables Jesus to speak to you and reveal things that you would not previously have valued or understood. Now Jesus can reveal new truths and spiritual blessings to you, using new picture parables.

Moving On

When you learned to rest in the Lord in the midst of storms, what opportunities were opened for you with Jesus? You can find out by asking:

Meeting Place: "Jesus, now that I have had this time of learning rest in my life, where can You take me that I couldn't otherwise get to?"

Q: "Why there, Lord?"

Q: "What would You like to do here, Lord?"

Gift: "Lord, what gift would You like to give me as we meet in this place?"

Q: "Why that gift?"

Feel: How does it feel to be in this new place with Jesus?

Q: "And Lord, through this experience and learning rest, do You have a new name for me?"

145

Q: "Why that, Lord?"

Journal what the Lord showed you, what He told you, any questions you have, and His responses, keeping in mind that a new name is a powerful thing.

LEARNING TO WALK ON WATER

(MATT 14:22-33)

Was there ever a time the Lord asked you to trust Him in the midst of a storm of life? To live by faith? To step out and do something that you know should have sunk you, but instead you survived, and maybe even thrived?

Journal: Spend some time pondering what life was like back then. Journal some memories, feelings, and experiences you had at that time.

Look: Peer over the side of the boat during that faith building time in your life; what was the water like then?

Look: Ask Jesus to allow you to look at this storm through His eyes. What does Jesus see when He looks at this "life storm," at this faith building time in your life?

Q: "Jesus, why does this storm look this way to You?"

Journal what Jesus says, and dialog with Him about it.

Stepping Over the Guard Rail

In every step of faith there comes a time when you cannot trust what you see or feel, but only what you sense in your heart the Lord is saying to you. So, in this "life storm," watch as the Lord steps over the side of the boat, walks on the water, and calls you over.

Look: Watch Jesus step over the side of the boat and turn to face you as He stands on the water.

Listen: What does Jesus want to say to you at this moment?

Journal what Jesus says, and dialog with Him about it.

Look: What is the expression on Jesus' face as you get ready to step out?

Look: What is the expression on Jesus' face as you step out?

Q: As you walk on the water toward Jesus, what new name would the Lord like to give you?

Q: Ask Jesus why that name.

Gift: "Jesus, do you have a gift, as your friend approaches on the water?"

Q: "Why that?"

Journal anything the Lord reveals to you.

Moving On

Q: "Lord, as I learned to walk by faith during this life storm with You, how did this change my life?"

Meeting Place: "Jesus, now that I have had this time of learning to walk by faith in my life, where can You take me that I couldn't otherwise go?"

Q: "Why there, Lord?"

Q: "What would You like to do there, Jesus?"

Gift: "Lord, what gift would You like to give me as we meet in this place?"

Q: "Why that gift?"

Feel: Take a moment and consider how it feels to be in this new place?

Journal anything the Lord showed you, told you, any questions you have, and the Lord's responses.

Week 30

WATCHING THE MASTER AND COMMANDER

(MATT 8:26-27)

We have all witnessed times of divine intervention. For you it may have been the situation that brought you to salvation, or possibly the time the Lord first spoke to you and you realized that He does speak today. Perhaps it was a divine healing or a miraculous encounter. In any case, there are times when Jesus has taken command in our lives and we have been able to watch the Master and Commander calm a life storm, or the lives of our friends or our church, in a miraculous way.

Ponder: Spend some time pondering that event, how you felt at the time, and what life was like just before the Lord's intervention.

Look: Thinking about that time in your life, peer over the side of the boat. How did things look just before the Lord's intervention?

Look: Now let's invite Jesus to "do His thing." Watch as the Lord looks out from the boat at that life storm. What is the expression on the Lord's face as He observes the sea?

Q: "Why do You have that expression, Jesus?"

Look: As Jesus observes this life storm, what does He want to say to it?

151

Look: Now, watch what happens as Jesus pronounces His words of life over the wind and waves.

Look: What is the expression on the Lord's face now?

Q: "Why that expression?"

Q: "Lord, why did You want to intervene in that life storm?"

Gift: "Lord, do You have a gift to give me now that You have intervened?"

Q: "Why that?"

Promise: "Lord, is there a promise You want me to receive from You?"

Journal anything the Lord showed you or told you, and dialog with the Lord about it.

Moving On

Q: "Lord as I experienced You commanding my life storm to be still, how did this change my life?"

Meeting Place: "Jesus, now that I have had this time of seeing Your power over my life storms, where can You take me that I couldn't otherwise go?"

Q: "Why there, Lord?"

Q: "What would You like to do there, Lord?"

Gift: "Lord, what gift would You like to give me as we meet in this place?

Why that?"

Feel: What does it feel like to meet the Lord in this new place?

Journal anything the Lord showed you or told you, any questions you have, and the Lord's responses.

Week 31

THE BOUNTY OF THE SEA

(LUKE 5:1-11)

There is a lot more to the sea than storms, just as there is a lot more to life than troubles. In fact, when Jesus first met His soon-to-be-famous fishermen, storms were the furthest things from their minds. What the future disciples were thinking about was not the sea, itself, but what was in it: fish.

A Time of Harvest

Think back to a time of favor in your life when God was opening doors for you, you were experiencing His manifest presence, or He was blessing you financially, physically, spiritually, etc.

Journal: Spend some time pondering what life was like then (or currently); journal some memories, feelings, and experiences you had at that time.

Look: Peer over the side of the boat at that time of favor. What was happening out on the water?

Look: Ask the Lord to allow you to look from His point of view.

The Lord's Heart: "Jesus, when You look out over the side of the boat and over the water during this time of favor in my life, what do You see and feel?"

Q: "Why do You see and feel that, Lord?"

Look: What is the expression on the Lord's face as He sees what He sees and feels what He feels?

Q: "Why that expression, Jesus?"

Moving On

Q: "Lord, as I learned to receive this favor and blessing from You, how did this change my life?"

Meeting Place: "Jesus, now that I have had this time of favor in my life, where can you take me that I couldn't otherwise go?"

Q: "Why there, Lord?"

Q: "What would You like to do there, Jesus?"

Gift: "Lord, what gift would You like to give me as we meet in this place?"

Q: "Why that gift?"

Feel: What does it feel like to be with the Lord in this new meeting place?

Journal anything the Lord showed you or told you, any questions you have, and the Lord's responses.

Week 32

APPROACHING THE THRONE BOLDLY

(HEB 4:16)

A story is told of a young prince who was instructed to wait in the castle. His father, the King, had been off to war, and rumors had spread that he was now returning with his army, captives, and treasure. Soon the king's army would be marching down the main road to the cheers of his people. The young prince peered out of the castle window, waiting expectantly to hear the sound of the drums and the boots marching, and catch a glimpse of his father, the king, in his royal robes.

As the army approached and the sound of cheering swelled, the young prince could stand it no longer; he ran down the steps of the castle, bolted out the gate, and pressed through the crowd to see his father. As he ran toward the king the guards shouted at him, "No one approaches the king!" But the king looked down and, upon seeing his son, signalled to his guards to let the boy through, for this boy was not just a subject: he was a son, and a prince. As it was true for the prince, so it is true for us: we also have a Father who is a King, who does not stop us from approaching Him in His royalty. And we can do so with confidence:

> Let us then approach the *throne of grace* with confidence, so that we may receive mercy and find grace to help us in our time of need. (Heb 4:16, NIV, italics added.)

Let's Approach This Throne of Grace!

Even as sons and daughters of the King, approaching His throne can be a little intimidating, for the throne our heavenly Father sits on flashes with lightening and rings with loud peals of thunder!49 But there is more: we find in Revelation 4:3 that this throne is encircled by a rainbow, and a rainbow is a symbol of promise and safety.

Look: As you approach the throne of grace with this encircling rainbow, what colors of the rainbow stand out to you?

Q: If God could cause one of those rainbow colors to come shining down on you as you approach the throne, what color would He pick?

Q: "Why that color, Lord?"

Promise: "Lord, do You have a promise that goes with this color?"

Since Hebrews 10:22 encourages us to draw near to God, it's time to take another step closer to that throne.

Look: If God could cause another one of the colors of that rainbow to come shining down on you, what would be the next color the Lord would pick?

Q: "Why that color, Lord?"

Gift: "Lord, do You have a gift that goes with this color?"

Q: "Why that gift?"

---

49   Rev 4:5.

Kings and Priests

As you approach this rainbow-encircled throne as a son or daughter, ponder Revelation 1:6:

> [He] has made us kings and priests to His God and Father, to Him be glory and dominion forever and ever. Amen. (NKJV)

Since you are a king and a priest, Jesus must have some kingly items for you, such as a royal robe, a crown, a sceptre, etc., and some priestly items for you as well, such as a priestly robe, a scroll, a staff, etc.

Look: As you approach, what kingly and/or priestly items would Jesus like to pass to you today?

Q: "Why those items, Lord?"

Q: "What do they represent?"

Promise: "Do You have a promise for me to go along with these items, Lord?"

Journal what the Lord has shown you and told you, and dialog with Him about it.

Week 33

SEATED IN THE HEAVENLIES WITH CHRIST

It may surprise you to learn that, reserved in the heavenlies with Christ, is a seat for you too! Jesus promised us that we would sit down beside Him as He sat down with His Father.

> And God raised us up with Christ and seated us with him in the heavenly realms in Christ Jesus. (Eph 2:6)

So, what would your seat look like today? Since a chair is a great symbol for what its function is, your seat could possibly look like:

- a recliner, to symbolize resting;

- a kitchen chair, to represent preparing to serve with the Lord;

- a throne, to symbolize authority;

- a footstool, to represent humility.[50]

Could it be possible that your seat in heaven is a kitchen chair? Some-day, when we move on to glory and we are finished with this world, I don't expect our throne to be changing into a kitchen chair. It is pretty clear in Revelation 3:21 we will sit with Jesus on His throne. Nonetheless, as the above verse states, we are seated with Christ in the heavenly realms while in this life, too—right now. Thus the chair is a

---

50   The style of chair does not impact the authority of where the chair is placed, which is in heaven. This chair will always function as a throne, but the Lord may change the style to indicate what He asking us to do with His authority in that moment.

161

great symbol of how the Lord teaches us to sit with Him in seasons of rest, service, authority, humility, etc. This symbol depicts the vital truth Christ is developing in us right now: that we are seated with Him.

Finding Your Seat

Think back to the last activation, step back into those colors of the rainbow, and put on your royal robe and kingly/priestly items that Jesus passed to you. Now, look around for Jesus' seat—and then for your seat.

Look: If Jesus had a seat for you to sit with Him in the heavenly places, what would it look like? What kind of chair would it be?

Q: Ask Jesus why your chair would look like that today.

Q: Would there be any precious jewels or symbols on your chair?

Q: Ask the Lord if your chair can change in its appearance, depending on what He is teaching you or what you are doing together. Why?

Look: Ask the Lord to show you some other ways your chair has looked in the past.

Q: "Why that look or style of chair, Lord?"

Q: "What were you doing in my life at that time, that made my chair look like that?"

Gift: "If I learn to sit with You in this chair, do You have a gift for me?"

Q: "Why that, Lord?"

Promise: "How about a promise, Jesus?"

Journal anything the Lord has spoken to you or shown you, and dialog with Him about it.

Week 34

DOING AS PRIESTS AND KINGS DO

(1 PET 2:9)

Whether the Lord has us on a simple kitchen chair, in a recliner, or on a throne, this seat in the heavens has a purpose. It is a place from which we can serve our God, as Revelation 1:6 says, as kings and priests. For, no matter what this chair looks like, this is a seat of authority given to us by God to see His will done on the earth; and, by watching what Jesus is doing on His throne, we can learn what we are supposed to do on ours. Since Hebrews 7:25 tells us that Jesus lives to make intercession, why not learn intercession from the best—Jesus, Himself?

Heavenly Intercession

Look: As Jesus sits on His throne, looking down on the earth, what is the expression on His face?

Q: "Lord, what are You watching for on the earth right now? What is it You want to do? Who do You want to touch?"

Look: Ask Jesus to allow you to see from your seat what He is looking at from His.

Q: "Lord, if You could change anything for this person, situation, or nation, what would You change?"

Q: "Would You show me what that change would look like?"

Look: Now, wearing your priestly and kingly garments and seated on your seat in the heavenlies, look where Jesus is looking and pray for the changes the Lord wants to see happen.

Look: After you have prayed for a little while, look back at Jesus on His throne. Now that you have interceded regarding what Jesus had on his heart, what is the expression on Jesus' face? How has it changed?

Q: "Lord, why do You have that expression, now that I have prayed that Your will would be done on earth as it is in heaven?"

Q: "Lord, if I could learn to sit beside You on my seat and pray what I see you praying, what would change and develop in my life as time goes by?"

Q: "Why that, Lord?"

Journal anything that the Lord has shown you or told you, and dialog with Him about it.

Week 35

PUTTING GLORY ASIDE

(MATT 2:11)

As we have sat beside Jesus on His throne, seeing Him in His majesty, involving ourselves in that majesty, it is a good time to remind ourselves what kind of King Jesus is: a humble one. Having a partial glimpse of the King in His glory, we may now be able to grasp, in some small measure, what Jesus actually gave up to come and walk among us by coming to this earth as a little baby. Therefore, with His majesty and glory in mind, let's spend some time before the cradle. Getting a feel for the vast disparity between these two symbols, Jesus' throne and His cradle, will give us a better understanding of what our King Jesus is really all about.

Becoming a Wiseman

Now, stand with our heavenly Father as He witnesses this scene of His Son Jesus with His earthly parents, Mary and Joseph:

> On coming to the house, they saw the child with his mother Mary, and they bowed down and worshiped him. Then they opened their treasures and presented him with gifts of gold and of incense and of myrrh. (Matt 2:11)

Look: As the Father looks at His son Jesus, now as a child with human parents, what is the expression on His face?

Q: "Father, why do You have that expression when You look at your Son, Jesus?"

The Father's Heart: "Father, when You think of Your Son being willing to lay down all His glory to come to earth as a baby, how does that make You feel?"

Gift: "If You were to give Your Son a gift today, Father, what would You give Him?"

Journal everything the Father tells you about His Son, Jesus, and dialog with Him about it.

The Gifts of the Magi

Look: As you are standing with the Father, watch the Magi present Jesus with their gifts of gold, frankincense, and myrrh. Talk with the Father about these gifts.

Q: "Father, these are strange presents for a young child. Why these three items, Father?"

Q: "What are they used for? What do they represent?"

Journal about these items with the Father, and dialog together about their meaning.

Week 36

GIVING YOUR GIFT
(MATT 2:11)

Think back to your last journal entry, when you were standing with the Father, looking at Jesus with His parents and the Magi, watching the gifts being given. If you could give Jesus a gift, what would you give Him? Having asked that question, it may be good to stop here, take a deep breath, and ponder. What does one give a King who has everything, and who has also given away everything to come to earth as a small child?

Getting to the Heart of the Matter

You have several choices here, all of which would help you get into your heart before you present your gift. A first helpful step is to think symbolically. For example, if you want to give Jesus all of your love, giving Him the gift of your heart would be appropriate. If you want to give Jesus a gift of service, reaching your hands toward Him would be fitting. If you desire to surrender your life, kneeling would be the symbol. Let's go deeper than that. You don't want to merely offer gestures here; you want to be authentic. Here are a few suggestions to help make the journey from the head to the heart:

1. Review your life and think about the times Jesus has met you, saved you, spoken to you, healed you, protected you, etc. What rises up in your heart as you ponder these encounters with Jesus?

2. Write a love letter to Jesus saying "thank you" for loving you so much He came and stepped into broken humanity to take your sins, and to offer us all eternal life. When you are done, journal His response to you.

3. After completing the first two steps, with your heart overflowing with thankfulness, think of a gift, or a number of gifts, that would be appropriate to give to the child Jesus. (Some of those I mentioned earlier would now be fitting.)

Looking at Jesus

Present your gift(s) to Jesus and tell Him why that gift.

Look: Look at the expression on Jesus' face as you present the gift.

Gift: Since Scripture says Jesus gave gifts to men,[51] does Jesus have a gift for you? Look to see!

Promise: Does Jesus have a promise for you?

Journal anything the Lord showed you or told you, and dialog with Him about it.

---

51   Eph 4:8.

Week 37

ROLLING WAVES

Deep calls to deep at the sound of your waterfalls: All your breakers and your waves have rolled over me. (Ps 42:7, NASB)

Have you ever stood on the shore of the ocean and watched the waves roll in? The sound of the water, the smell of the sea brine in the air, the sight of the majestic waves rising up out of the sea, rolling along before curling in and crashing down on the beach. The whole experience is almost a musical score, a dance, a rising crescendo, and then a calm, all repeating again and again—seemingly for eternity.

In the midst of these dancing waves and musical score of nature, I find the heartbeat of the Father. I am reminded that God loves His creation; that He has a rhythm to the way He does things. The Father is never rushed or hurried, and God, despite my own fears and worries, is in control. Indeed, there is a lot to be learned by watching the waves roll in.

Standing at the Shore and Watching the Waves

Stand with Jesus at the water's edge and ask Jesus to let the waves of God's love roll in.

Look: If a wave of God's love would come rolling right up to the beach, what would it look like?

Q: What color would a wave of God's love be?

Q: How big would a wave of God's love be?

Listen: What would it sound like?

Keep looking until the wave comes rolling right up the beach and crashes into you!

Feel: What does it feel like to have a wave of God's love crash right into you and soak you from head to toe?

Gift: When waves come rolling in, they often leave things deposited along the beach. If the Father could leave a gift behind for you as the wave recedes, what would you find at your feet from the Father?

Q: "Why that gift, Father?"

Promise: Having encountered the wave and then the gift, let's turn to Jesus and ask Him if He has a promise for you.

Journal what the Lord has shown you, and dialog with Him about it.

Week 38

THE NEXT WAVE

There are a lot of lessons when we are learning to look with our spiritual eyes, and one of them is to keep looking! We find Daniel doing just that,[52] as well as Zechariah. In fact, Zechariah is told by an angel to keep looking, and he does so.[53] This is good advice for us as well. We can learn to keep looking by not merely picturing the wave itself, but also watching the wave's action. With this in mind, stand with Jesus at the water's edge and ask Him to let another wave roll all the way in to the beach—a wave of God's forgiveness.

Look: If a wave of God's forgiveness could come rolling up to the beach, what would it look like?

Q: What color would a wave of God's forgiveness be?

Q: How big would a wave of forgiveness be?

Listen: What would it sound like?

Keep looking until the wave crashes right into you!

Feel: What does it feel like to have a wave of God's forgiveness crash right into you and soak you from head to toe?

---

52   Dan 8:15.
53   Zech 4:1; 5:5.

Look: Here is a great way to keep looking in the Spirit—start with your toes and work your way up. Look to see what the wave of God's forgiveness has done for you.

Q: What has happened to your feet?

Q: What has happened to your legs?

Q: What has happened to your arms?

Q: What has happened to your chest?

Look: What is the look on Jesus' face after looking to see the effects of this wave?

Q: "Why that look, Jesus?"

Journal what the Lord has shown and told you, and dialog with Him about it.

Week 39

WAVES OF GLORY!

For the earth will be filled with the knowledge of the
glory of the Lord, as the waters cover the sea. (Hab 2:14)

In Habakkuk 2:1-2, we find Habakkuk "looking to see" what the Lord
would say to him. While Habakkuk is looking, we find the above
description of the glory of the Lord being like water covering the sea.
So what would a wave of glory be like?

Standing at the Shore and Watching the Waves

Stand with Jesus at the water's edge and ask Jesus to let a wave of God's
glory roll in, right up to the beach.

Look: If a wave of God's glory could come rolling in, what would it
look like?

Q: How big would a wave of glory be?

Q: What color would a wave of God's glory be?

Listen: What would it sound like?

Keep looking until the wave comes rolling right in and crashes right
over you!

Feel: What does it feel like to have a wave of God's glory crash right
into you and soak you from head to toe?

Deep Calls to Deep

There is much more going on in the ocean than just waves as seen on the surface: there are also deep places. In our opening verse, we are also told that, "Deep calls to deep." [54] In the deep places of the oceans there are many treasures, and people spend a lot of time and money searching for them. This being the case, what treasure would we find in Jesus if we didn't just wait for God's waves of glory to come to us? What if we pursue, dive in, and see what God has waiting for us in the deep places in the ocean of His glory?

Diving In

Dive into that wave of glory and swim down into the depths with Jesus. What a treasure Jesus has waiting down there for you! Keep looking until you find it!

Look: What is it like to swim through a wave of glory? What do you see?

Feel: What do you feel?

Gift: What about a gift? Is there treasure down there? Do you see it?

Journal what the Lord has shown you and dialog with Him about it.

---

54   Ps 42:7.

Week 40

LET THE WAVES KEEP ROLLING IN

If you have ever taken a vacation at the ocean, I am sure you remember not wanting the vacation to end! And it is the same when meeting Jesus by the sea of God's love. Fortunately for us, we don't ever have to leave this place of impartation; we can come back again and again. And in fact, before we go, we should do one more thing: keep looking. Let's stand on the seashore with Jesus and let the waves do what they do best: keep coming in, over and over again.

On a Roll

Let's stand with Jesus, our feet in the water, and let the waves of the Father wash over us, waves of love, peace, joy, humility, kindness, mercy, power, healing, etc., wave after wave of the good things God has for us.

Look: Stand with Jesus, look out at the waves, and watch a wave as it rolls in.

Q: What does it look like? What color is it?

Gift: What could this wave contain from the Father for you? Peace, joy, healing, power, mercy, etc.? Turn to Jesus and ask Him.

Look: What is the look on Jesus' face as the wave approaches?

Feel: What does it feel like to let that wave wash over you?

Look: With Jesus, watch the next wave come in.

Promise: "Jesus, as I watch this wave from Your Father roll in, does it carry a promise?"

Q: Why that promise, Lord?

Look: What is the look on Jesus' face as the wave approaches?

Feel: What does it feel like to let that wave wash over you?

Look: With Jesus, watch the next wave come in.

Gift: "Jesus, as I watch this wave from Your Father roll in, does it carry a gift from Your Father?"

Q: "What that gift, Lord?"

Look: What is the look on Jesus' face as the wave approaches?

Feel: What does it feel like to let that wave wash over you?

Now, keep it up! Wave after wave, talking with Jesus, looking at His face, letting the love of the Father wash over you.

One last thought:

If you keep meeting with Jesus by the sea of the Father's love, and you keep letting the Lord fill you with His waves of love, what is going to change for you as time goes by? John 16:13 says that the Holy Spirit will show you what is to come; so, if you keep allowing the Father to wash over you with His waves of love, what is going to change for you after a month? Two months? Two years? Five years? Ask Jesus to fast-forward the picture, and watch what changes and grows as you continue to allow the Lord to wash over you with His love, mercy, and grace.

Journal everything the Lord has shown you and told you, and dialog with Him about it.

Week 41

YOUR PLACE OR MINE
(1 COR 1:9)

Hopefully, as you have worked your way through this journal, you have come across a few favorite meeting places. These places with the Lord are always available to you. If you need a restful place, perhaps being by the waves would be perfect; a powerful place could find you back at the throne, etc. You can always go back and meet with Jesus at any of the earlier meeting places anytime you want.

With this in mind, I would like to re-introduce the meeting place activation you did in the opening section of the book. Learning to have fellowship with Jesus is vital to your spiritual life, and having many good meeting places to enjoy and explore will add excitement and intimacy to your conversations with Jesus.

Your Meeting Place

Think of a meeting place that would be perfect for you today. Maybe you have had a stressful day, so being by the ocean may be perfect; or possibly you need some time with the Father, so maybe the story of the prodigal is just right for you. Having pondered your day, what would be the perfect meeting place for you and Jesus?

Look: Picture that place and wander around it with Jesus; tell Him why this is the perfect place for you today.

Jesus' Place

You now know what you have in your own heart regarding the perfect place to meet Jesus. What would Jesus think is the perfect place to meet you? IT COULD BE THE EXACT SAME PLACE, BUT NOT NECESSARILY. ASK HIM.

Look: "Jesus, if You were to pick the place to meet me today, what place would You pick? Would You pick the same place or a different place?"

Q: "Why this place, Lord?" (Now, if you want, you can hang out with Jesus in your place, His place, or spend some time in both places!)

Q: "Jesus, what would You like to do in this place?"

Q: "Why that, Lord?"

Gift: "Do You have a gift for me here, Lord?"

Promise: "How about a promise?"

Q: "Lord, if I keep meeting You in this place, what is going to change as time goes by? Fast-forward this picture into the future. Lord, what is going to change after a year? Two years? Five years? Ten years?"

Q: "Why those changes, Lord?"

Journal anything the Lord showed or told you, and dialog with Jesus about it.

Week 42

PUTTING ON THE ARMOR

(EPH 6:13-17)

Keep the conversation with Jesus going from last week, and meet with Jesus in that meeting place again, but this time add the "armor of God."

Ephesians 6:13-17 gives us a list of the armor and the uses of the specific pieces. Let's review that list:

helmet of salvation

breastplate of righteousness

belt of truth

shoes of the gospel of peace

shield of faith

sword of the Spirit

Look: Having reviewed the various pieces of armor, lay them out in front of you in your meeting place and ask Jesus to look them over.

Now, think about your day. If you were to pick the piece of armor you think you need the most, which piece would you pick? (E.g., if you had a stressful day, you might want those shoes of peace; or perhaps your faith has been a bit shaken, so the shield of faith may be the perfect item.)

Present the piece of armor you think you need the most to Jesus and tell Him why that would be the perfect piece of armor for today.

Jesus Picks

Look: "Jesus, You know which piece of armor I would choose today. Lord, if you had the choice and You were to pick the piece of armor you think I need the most at this moment, which piece would You pick?"

Q: "Would You pick the same piece or a different piece?"

Q: "Why would You choose that piece of armor, Lord?"

Promise: Ask Jesus now to come and place all the pieces of armor on you and, while He is doing that, give you a promise with every piece:

The promise for the helmet of salvation is _____

The promise for the breastplate of righteousness is _____

The promise for the belt of truth is_____

The promise for the shoes of the gospel of peace is _____

The promise for the shield of faith is _____

The promise for the sword of the spirit _____

Q: "Why these promises for these items, Lord?"

Q: "Lord, if I choose to wear this armor daily, where would You take me and what would You show me that You couldn't before?"

Q: "Why there, Lord?"

Journal anything the Lord showed you or told you, and dialog with Jesus about it.

Week 43

ALL DRESSED UP AND SOMEWHERE TO GO

Have you ever had a moment when you were all dressed up and your parents or your significant other stood back, looked you up and down and, with a smile said, "You look great!" Believe it or not, that is just how Jesus feels when He looks at you wearing His armor.

Step back into this meeting place again, but this time find out what is on the Lord's heart when He sees you in the armor He has given you.

Look: Since 1 Corinthians 2:16 says we have the mind of Christ, invite Jesus into this scene where you are standing, wearing your armor, and holding the shield and sword. Notice where Jesus chooses to stand, sit, or lean.

Look: What is the expression on Jesus' face when He looks at you?

Q: "Why that expression, Lord?"

Then, ask Jesus to allow you to stand in His shoes and look through His eyes. When Jesus sees you wearing the armor and holding the sword and shield, what does He see? How does He feel? Do you look like a servant or a son, from His point of view?

Q: "Why do You see me like that, Jesus?"

The Lord's Heart: "Why do You feel like that when you look at me in my armor?"

Future View of You and Your Armor

Since John 16:13 tells us the Holy Spirit can show us what is to come, ask Jesus to fast-forward into the future this picture of you wearing the armor and holding the shield and sword.

Q: "Lord, if I receive this armor from You, and I keep it on, what is going to change for me?"

Q: "Where do we go from here?"

Q: "How am I going to grow and move forward?"

Look: Now let the Holy Spirit fast-forward this into the future a year, two years, five years, ten years. What changes? What develops?

Journal all of the changes and record all you see, sense, and feel.

Jesus Point of View of Your Future

Now that the Holy Spirit has fast-forward this picture of you into the future, step into Jesus' shoes and look through His eyes one more time. What does Jesus see and feel when He looks at you in this future time, having worn this armor and carried this sword and shield over a number of years? What has changed from Jesus' point of view?

Look: "Jesus, when You look at me from Your point of view, having carried the armor, and grown over a number years, how do I look to You now?"

The Lord's Heart: "How does what You see make you feel?"

Q: "Jesus, after seeing me in this armor and showing me how I am going to grow and mature, do You have a new name for me?"

Q: "Why that name, Jesus?

Gift: "Would You have a gift for me as well?"

Q: "Why that, Lord?"

Journal anything that the Lord has shown you or told you, and spend some time discussing it together.

Week 44

DISCOVERING THE ANOINTING ON YOUR ARMOR

We discussed earlier in this journal that when God gives us something, it is not merely an image, it is something that carries an "anointing." In other words, it is a specific gift or fruit of the Holy Spirit we need for that moment. With this in mind, we want to do more with the armor than look at it; we want to take Paul's advice in Ephesians 6:13 and "put it on" by discerning what anointing these pieces of armor contain. To do that, go back to week 13 and do the same activation, but this time, insert the pieces of the armor of God instead of the ring, robe, and shoes.

Week 45

THE TIME CAPSULE

Have you heard of a time capsule? It is a chest or vault buried with relics of the present for people in the future to discover. Sometimes they are put into the cornerstone of a building. In a time capsule are things from a long time ago that were precious to people from an earlier era. When it is opened decades or centuries later, you get to see what was considered valuable at that earlier time. Just as time capsules are placed in cornerstones of buildings, so also with Jesus, our cornerstone (Eph 2:20). He has blessings for you that have been stored up in Him from the past, and even for your family line. For, when God blesses people and gives gifts to them, time may go by, but He never forgets.

> He remembers his covenant forever, the word he commanded, for a thousand generations. (Ps 105:8)

Many blessings and giftings from God tend to pass along family lines. For example, your mother may have been musical, as was her mother. Or your father may have been good at math, and his father as well. This would hold true for all of the gifts that can be passed along: music, art, writing, speaking, math, building, etc. Spiritual giftings such as worship, having the heart of a pastor, the ability to dream, etc., can pass along family lines as well. Unfortunately, gifts from God can also get lost if people don't value them. One good example is the gift of dreams. I work a lot with dreams, which are a great blessing to many people, but what if the members of a family have the gift of dreaming but they don't value dreams? What if that lack of value is passed along from generation to generation? The gifting can go dormant. That same lack of value leading to dormancy may hold true for music, art, finances, leadership, or any gifting. If a family does not value what God has given, that gift can be lost. Even so, God has not forgotten the promises He made at an earlier time, or the gifts He gave—they are all safe inside His time capsule—Himself.[55] He knows the good gifts He has for you, and He wants you to have them. You may not even know your family, but that doesn't matter, because God knows. Even if your family messed it up, God's gifts are still available, and He still wants to pass those good gifts and blessings along to you.[56] So ask Jesus to place a time capsule in front of you that would represent the good gifts and blessings He has put in your family line.

Look: What does the time capsule look like? A bank vault? A treasure chest? Something else?

Q: Are there any precious stones or symbols on your time capsule?

Promise: Could there be a promise from the Lord written on it?

Q: Ask Jesus why your capsule looks like it does.

Thinking Symbolically

Before you ask the Lord to open the time capsule, take a moment to switch to Jesus' favorite teaching language: picture parables. For, in this time capsule, there will be symbolic items, which will need to be interpreted. For example, the gift of music may be symbolized by a guitar, the gift of writing by a pen, the gift of finances by a gold coin, the gift of speaking by a microphone, the gift of working with children by the sound of children's laughter, etc.

Ponder: Think of three things you are good at and the symbols that could represent them. Then, pass those symbolic items to Jesus to see what He would like to say to you about them. Spend some time journaling what the Lord tells you.

---

55   Rom 11:36.
56   Jas 5:17.

Opening the Capsule

You now know what your time capsule looks like, and have spent a little time pondering a few giftings in your life you know the Lord has already given you. What else does Jesus have for you in that time capsule?

Gift: "Jesus, would You open the time capsule, reach inside, and bring out a gift that You have been keeping safe for me?"

Q: What would be the first gift Jesus would bring out?

Q: What would be the second gift Jesus would bring out?

Q: The third gift?

Q: "Jesus, why these items? What do they represent?"

Q: "Do You have anything else in there for me today, Jesus?"

Promise: Does the Lord have a promise for you to go with these gifts?

Journal and dialog with the Lord about all that He told you and showed you.

Week 46

FROM DORMANCY TO LIFE

Seeds that have been dormant for thousands of years, have been proven to be able to come back to life[57]—just like gifts from your time capsule! These gifts from God just need a little love and care.

Now that you have received some of the gifts the Lord has been keeping safe in your time capsule, it is time to give them some love and care by pondering how they will affect your life. As you accept these gifts from Jesus, you are going to grow, change, and develop new abilities you may have never thought possible. Dormant seeds can spring to life rather quickly!

Look: Place the gifts from the time capsule in front of you and Jesus.

Q: Ask Jesus which item He would like to talk with you about first.

Journal: Spend some time writing and dialoging back and forth with Jesus about each item. Ask Jesus any questions you have and let Him respond.

Look: Ask Jesus to allow you to look at these gifts from His point of view. When He looks at these items from the times capsule, what does He see?

The Lord's Heart: How does Jesus feel about each item?

57   *Wikipedia*, s.v. "Oldest Viable Seed," accessed Jan 12, 2014, http://en.wikipedia.org/wiki/Oldest_viable_seed.

Q: "Jesus, why do You see these items and feel for these items the way you do?"

Journal anything the Lord shows you or tells you.

What is to Come

Isaiah 55:9-11 tells us that when God gives a blessing, it is going to change and grow. With that in mind, pick up the first item and ask the Lord this question:

Q: "Lord, if I choose to receive this gift from You and let it live in my life, what is going to change in a year? Two years? Five years? Fast-forward the picture, Lord."

Q: "Lord, why do You see those kinds of changes in my life if I receive this gift from You?"

Ponder: Do the same with each item that the Lord gave you.

Journal and dialog with the Lord about everything He showed you and told you.

Checking the Anointing

As you can imagine, there is a lot more we can do with these items from the time capsule. One idea would be to check what anointing each item carries from the Lord. To do so, go back to week 13 and insert each item from the time capsule in place of the ring, robe, and shoes.

Week 47

PASSING THE BLESSINGS FORWARD

You have received some blessings and giftings that may have been dormant in your family line for a long time, but that doesn't mean those gifts need to stay dormant for the rest of your family. You can ask Jesus to pass them on to your children or other family members! Then, by watching what Jesus does with these gifts for the people you love, you can learn how to pray the Lord's will for them.

Look: Picture a meeting place with you and Jesus. What would be the perfect place? The ocean? The boat? The pasture? Somewhere else?

Look: Where would Jesus be in this meeting place? What would He be doing?

Look: Invite into that meeting place the various members of your family, one at a time, to whom the Lord would like to pass along the gifts from the time capsule.

Look: Watch the Lord as He passes out the various gifts to each person.

Q: Ask the Lord why He gave each person that particular gift (and keep in mind that any of the gifts could be given to any members of the family).

Promise: "Lord, do You have a promise for each person that goes with that gift?"

Q: "Why that promise for that person, Lord?"

Journal and dialog with the Lord about everything that He showed you and told you.

Note: The Lord may have other gifts for the members of your family in the time capsule. Ask Jesus to bring the time capsule into the meeting place and see if He has anything else He would like to bring out for them.

Week 48

THE KNOCK ON THE DOOR OF YOUR HEART

I have a cat named Fitzimpin, and she has a real problem with closed doors: inside doors, outside doors, bedroom doors, bathroom doors—if the door is closed, Fitzy is offended and wants in. She will meow, scratch, put her paw under the door, whatever it takes to get that door open. And, as much as I hate to admit it, she usually gets her way. But, as I have watched Fitzy's persistence and confidence that I will listen to her and open the door, the Lord has taught me through this. Here is the verse that the Lord brings to my mind often:

> Here I am! I stand at the door and knock. If anyone hears my voice and *opens the door*, I will come in and eat with him, and he with me. (Rev 3:20, italics added.)

So now, when my cat is at my door, knowing that in the end I will let her in, I remind myself that Jesus, Himself, stands at the door of my heart and knocks: He wants in as well. With this in mind, to fellowship with Jesus, often all we need to do is listen for the knock the Lord promised, and open the door of our hearts.

The Door

Look: What would the door of your heart look like today? Would it be an old fashioned door or a new, modern one? Maybe your door is more of an archway or a gate. Look to see what type of door the Lord would put in front of you today.

Q: Does your door have any particular colors, symbols, or patterns?

Promise: Ask the Lord to write a promise on your door.

Q: "Jesus, why does the door of my heart look like this today?"

Q: "Why have You placed this promise on my door, Jesus?"

The Knock

Ask Jesus to knock on the door of Your heart:

Listen: What does the Lord's knock sound like? Loud? Quiet? Rhythmic? Tentative?

Feel: How does it feel to have the Lord knock on the door of your heart? Powerful? Peaceful?

Journal: Ask Jesus why His knock sounds and feels that way, and dialog with Him about it.

An Open Door

Look: Open the door of your heart and invite Jesus in.

Look: What is the expression on His face?

Q: "Jesus, why did You knock on the door of my heart?"

Gift: "Is there a gift You would like to give me, Lord?"

Q: "Why that gift?"

Look: As the Lord steps through your door at your invitation, what is going on in your heart? How does that look? How does that feel?

Journal everything that the Lord showed you and told you, and dialog with Him about it.

Note: Whether you are feeling great or not so great, go back, picture the door of your heart, and listen for the Lord's knock. Take the Lord up on His promise to come and knock on your door.

Week 49

JESUS THE DOORKEEPER

As a child, closed doors were intriguing. Christmas presents were hidden behind closed doors; on late summer evenings my bike was behind a closed door; and all the food I could eat was on the other side of the refrigerator door. I even think that this childlike fascination continued into my teenage years. In the airplane, what was it like on the other side of the cockpit door? At the theatre, what were the actors busy doing on the other side of the stage door?

Fortunately for us, Jesus likes to open doors:

> Ask and it will be given to you; seek and you will find; *knock and the door will be opened to you.* For everyone who asks receives; he who seeks finds; *and to him who knocks, the door will be opened.* (Matt 7:7-8, italics added.)

Wouldn't it be wonderful if Jesus was to put a door in front of you today that will allow you to meet Him anywhere, anytime? Jesus could take you where he wants you to go, show you what He wants you to see, and teach you what He wants you to learn at any moment. It just takes knocking on the Lord's door.

Pondering the Lord's Door

The Bible describes all kinds of doors and gates: the ancient gate in Psalm 24, the gates made of pearls in Revelation 21:21, the sheepfold door in John 10, etc. Having an endless variety of doors available to us, if the Lord was to put a door or gate in front of you today that would allow you to go with Him anywhere He would like to take you, what would it look like?

Look: Picture a door in front of you. What is it like? Is it big or small? Plain or ornate?

Q: Ask Jesus why His door for you looks like it does.

Look: What is the expression on Jesus' face as you examine His door?

Listen: Put your ear to the door. What do you hear?

Q: Jesus has a perfect garment for you to wear for the other side of the door; ask Jesus for it.

Gift: If Jesus had a gift for you, before you go through the door, what would it be?

Q: Ask Jesus why that gift.

Stepping into Jesus' Shoes

Since we have the mind of Christ,[58] and we can abide in Christ,[59] ask the Lord to allow you to step into His shoes and look through His eyes. When Jesus looks at this door, what does He see? What does He feel? What does He hear?

Ponder: Since there is an endless variety of doors the Lord could put in front of you, there is probably an endless possibility of places He would like to take you. Take a few moments and ponder what Jesus

---

58   1 Cor 2:16.
59   John 15:7.

could show you and teach you by walking through the doors He presents to you.

Journal and dialog with the Lord about all of the above.

Note: This is another great activation to come back to again and again. By picturing a door with the Lord, we are illustrating our desire to step into His will. By opening the door, the Lord is illustrating His desire to have us see what He is doing, give us access to the throne room, and train us in the things of the Spirit.

Week 50

STEPPING THROUGH THE DOOR

(REV 4:1)

"Come with me, I want to show you something!" This is always an intriguing thing for a friend to say. Usually it is done in confidence; there is something they don't want anyone else to see. We are brought into a special trust and given a special place as confidants. It is the same with the Lord: He has special treasures He wants to show us as His confidants. For example, when John saw the door open in heaven, "Come up here!" was the next thing he heard.[60] Another example of God taking His confidants somewhere special is when Jesus took Peter, James, and John up the Mount of Transfiguration with Him to reveal His glory.[61] Just as the Lord pulled His friends aside to reveal a secret, He wants to do the same for you—on the other side of the door.

Ponder last week's journal entry. Call to mind everything the Lord showed you and told you about His door. Ponder some of the possible places Jesus may take you, and prepare to step through the door.

Stepping Through

Q: As you stand before the door with Jesus, all dressed up and ready to go, what would Jesus like to say to you as He opens the door?

---

60   Rev 4:1.
61   Matt 17:1-9.

Look: What do you see as you go through the door with Jesus?

Listen: What do you hear as you go through the door with Jesus?

Feel: What do you feel as you go through the door with Jesus?

Look: Where has Jesus taken you? What does it look like?

Look: What is the look on Jesus' face as He watches you examine this new place?

Q: "Jesus, why this place?"

Look: "Is there anything specific You wish me to see?"

Q: "Is there anything You would like to do here?"

Q: "Jesus, is there anything You would like to tell me while we are here together?"

Look: Psalm 91:1 tells us that Jesus can meet us in a hidden, sheltered, secret place. Is there a secret place here, just for you and Jesus? Go with Jesus and find it!

Journal and dialog with the Lord concerning the things He has shown you and told you.

Week 51

OUT AND ABOUT WITH JESUS

Jesus loves movement. "Come up here," implies moving from where we are to where Jesus would like to meet us.[62] In Matthew 11:28, Jesus says, "Come to me." This desire for motion is also typified by Ezekiel in his vision, when he was told to dig through the wall to find a doorway and walk through it;[63] Jeremiah when he was told to go to the potters shed;[64] and John hearing a voice behind him, telling him to turn around to see the vision (which wasn't happening in front of him, but behind him).[65] To put it succinctly, there is a lot more to see if we keep looking. Therefore, in keeping with what we find in Scripture, we shouldn't treat vision as if it is on a flat television screen; we need to look up, down, and all around—we need to embrace movement. This being the case, go back through your door with Jesus to your meeting place and look around, using the principle of movement, to see things you may have missed.

Look: Look around for Jesus. Where would He be? What would He be doing? Go and join Him.

Q: Is there anything else Jesus would like to show you in this place? Take a moment to look up, down, right, left, and behind you. What do you see?

Listen: Do you hear anything you didn't hear before?

---

62   Rev 4:1.
63   Ezek 8:8.
64   Jer 18:2.
65   Rev 1:12.

Q: Ask Jesus if He would like to give you a tour around to show you and talk with you about anything new that you saw or heard.

Doing What You See the Father Doing

While you are with Jesus in this place and you are practicing looking and moving about, would the Father be here somewhere?

Q: "Jesus, I know You only do what You see Your Father doing; would You take me to where Your Father is?"

Look: Go with Jesus as He takes You to meet His Father. Look to see what is happening.

Q: "Father, what would You like to tell me about Your Son, Jesus?"

Q: "Father, what would You like to say to me?"

Q: "Father, do You have a new name for me? Why that name?"

Journal and dialog with Jesus about anything you saw or heard.

Week 52

TOUCHING THE HEART OF THE FATHER

Near the beginning of this journal we journeyed to the Father's house on the prodigal's road. We have come a long way since then, working through past issues on the boat, accepting our ability to be in the Spirit with our wings, and standing in authority with our armor. Now, keeping in mind what we have experienced and accomplished, it is time, again, to approach the glorious Father, as Paul describes Him in Ephesians 1:17. But this time, let's meet Him at home.

> In my Father's house are many rooms; if it were not so, I would have told you. I am going there to prepare a place for you. (John 14:2)

Is it possible to see the Father's house? Of course! But keep in mind the point of 1 Corinthians 13:12, "We see in a mirror, dimly, but then face to face." The word "dimly" in this passage is the Greek word for "enigma," meaning a puzzle or riddle. The parallel word in Hebrew, *chiydah*, was also used in the Old Testament when God spoke in symbols that needed to be interpreted.[66] In this life, we can see things from the Lord in riddles and parables, but there will come a day, when we are in heaven, when we won't need this language any more.[67] At the present time, Father may explain something to us about His house by showing us His house as a cabin in the woods, representing intimacy and peace; or possibly as a giant marble palace, representing authority and royalty. As far as symbols of what the Father's house would represent, both of these are true. But what does His house really look like? For that

---

66   Num 12:8; Jud 14:12; Prov 1:6; Hab 2:6.
67   To gain a clear understanding of the Lord's reasons for using symbolic language, please read my book *If This Were a Dream, What Would it Mean?*

answer, we may have to wait until we can see face to face. For now, we are to see in parable pictures.

Going to the Father's House

With that in mind, ask Jesus to bring you to His Father for a blessing.

Look: John 14:1 tells us that in our Father's house are many rooms, and it is in this house Jesus prepares a place for us. Ask Jesus to take you to the Father's house now to meet with the Father.

Look: What does the Father's house look like?

Feel: What does it feel like?

Q: Where do you see the Father?

Look: What is the expression on His face when He sees you?

Look: Ask the Father to put His hand on your heart and give you a blessing.

Feel: Now stretch your hand out to the Father and put your hand on His heart.

Look: What is the look on the Father's face as you stretch your hand toward Him?

Feel: What does it feel like to have your hand on the Father's heart?

Q: As you feel the heartbeat of the Father, what does it say to you?

Q: As you have your hand on the Father's heart, what flows from the Father into you?

Journal anything you saw or were told, and dialog it all out with Jesus and the Father.

JOURNAL ENTRY EXAMPLES

One reason I am including these journal entries in the back of the book is that I want you to get a feel for people's different styles. Because God has made us all unique, we all interact with Him in our own unique ways. For instance, in Azaleah's journal below, you will notice that "feeling" is her primary connection point with the Lord, through which all of the other forms of communication with the Lord follow. First, Azaleah feels or senses what God is imparting, for example, peace, love, power, or rest, and then the pictures, impressions, and thoughts flow.

As Azaleah is a friend of mine, I had a bit of a chuckle reading her journal entry. At one point Azaleah declares, "I just want to go away and hear what He has to say instead of typing!" That is so Azaleah. She is so sensitive to the Holy Spirit and feels His presence so easily that she has to stop typing. And some of you may be just like Azaleah.

As you read Azaleah's journal entry, pay attention to how often the word "feel" (or descriptive words about feeling) make an appearance. By doing so, you are observing how Azaleah's gift mix works when she encounters the Lord, and you get a taste of her style as she explains her experience.

Azeleah's Journal for Week 19: Pondering the Wind of the Spirit

When I think of the breath of God, the first thing I feel is the comfort of the wind on my skin, and His breath smelling like the mix of fresh dew in the morning and sea air blowing off the ocean. It feels like home. It fills me and gives me extraordinary "being," peace, stillness, and comfort. It feels as if I'm present with Him. My spirit settles in and I just "am." I'm aware of His Presence, and I can see flowers shining radiantly as if to say, "Aren't I beautiful? I'm radiant, and that's just how I'm created." The atmosphere is brighter, clearer, peaceful.

Each breath of the Spirit grows a sensitivity to how He is communicating to me. The color is invisible and clean, like He is invisible and clean, illustrating how knowledge cannot contain His being.

The second breath is slow and calming—a slow wind, a slow breath. It's as if He is tickling me and making me laugh with a child's joy.

The third breath is constant, warm, and wafting, comforting my spirit; a heavenly scent begins to descend.

The fourth breath, my muscles relax, and the concerns of the day begin to melt; He begins to call my name, "Azaleah, Azaleah, Azaleah."

The fifth breath, He asks me, "What are you doing?" I respond, "Talking to you, Lord". (My typing is slower and it's hard for me to do these exercises, because I just want to go away and hear what He has to say, instead of typing!)

The sixth breath, He says, "This isn't just an exercise—this is Me!"

The sound I heard with the first breath is a slow wind blowing softly. What is growing is comfort, and the normality of His peace and presence, a stillness, an awareness that He is God. I just want to go with the flow, instead of answering all the questions. I just want to hear the sounds of His breath that stills my soul, and is gentle and warm wafting on my skin. It is life giving and fills me with Himself. The smell is something never smelt on earth, it's like a scent of sweetness, not even quite floral—the scent of God. Each time He breathes on me, there's a greater assurance that He is here, He is ever-present, and I feel assured and secure. He feels very close and I feel content, with a constant aura of His Presence surrounding me.

Lord, why are you changing me this way? I hear Him say, "Remember, daughter, My promises are never broken. I will never leave or forsake you. You can feel centered all the time in any circumstance, because I AM your Center. You never have to be concerned, feel afraid, or ever feel abandoned. I am with you always in every arena. You never need to be insecure or feel the rug is being pulled out from under you. I never do that, though you may have experienced that from men. You can trust that when I am with you, it is not a false word, a false act, but it is true and you can trust in Me. Though circumstances around you change, My breath will continue to breathe over you so you will know I am with you."

Thanks, Lord, for allowing me to feel your presence through Your breath. You know I am a feeler-senser, and You know I need to feel You are here right beside me. This gives me peace, reassurance, a sense of being loved on, and a memory that You were there from the beginning when I was a little girl on the beach, feeling the same wind of Your Spirit. You, Lord, feel like home.

Adria's Entry

Adria is very different from Azaleah. Adria is a scholar with a Master's degree in Old Testament, and she is incredibly visual. In fact, I would almost say Adria has a photographic memory. It is no surprise that Adria's encountering begins with picturing, and then moves on to a theological explanation of what she is seeing. That is just so Adria!

You will probably realize pretty quickly that Adria is working through some chronic pain issues (in her discussion with the Lord), and what He wants her to learn through them.

Adria's Journal for Week 26: The Boat

Day 1:

Me: My boat would be a small skiff, barely large enough for two. There might be oars, but I can't use them. (My arms would hurt if I tried). If anyone does use the oars, it's Jesus. We're sitting out there on the water alone, facing one another. Sometimes I can see Him, sometimes I can't. Sometimes I feel as if we're going in circles; most of the time, I feel as if we're not moving at all—as if we're adrift. The water is still, slightly rippling in the breeze. It looks as if we're close to the shore, by a weeping willow tree, but far enough away from the bank that I cannot touch it—not very adventurous. The sky has lots of clouds; perhaps it is a solid sheet of cloud, but it is not dark. The plants look as if they're hibernating for the winter, though there is no snow. It is cool, but not cold.

Jesus: *You may feel as if you're going nowhere, but you're being gently blown and nudged along by the Spirit. This is a place to go slowly, otherwise the waters [your life] will get all stirred up and muddy, and the light won't be able to reach through to the bottom. There is a lot of peace here—you are not ruffled or upset by every circumstance that blows your way. I'm with you in the boat, though you don't always see Me, and My angels come to visit you as well. This is a journey that a person can only take alone with Me. I like all of this undivided attention alone with you. I am teaching you many things, including how to be with yourself so you can experience yourself in a way that will enable you to appreciate yourself. You feel as if you've been in*

220

this boat forever, but that's because you keep thinking about the destination you want to get to, not the journey. Learn from Me to enjoy the journey more—savor the rest, peace, and undistracted time we have together. This is a time of carefully crafted beauty. I am carefully crafting beautiful things in you so you will have a rich treasure inside to share with others. You may feel sad, lonely, and adrift, but you'll reach the fair havens eventually, and there will be much rejoicing. Many people will welcome you to shore—led by those you look up to.

My promise to you is that we will reach the haven waiting for you. In the meantime, I am with you, and I will always be with you.

Me: It's late and I'm really tired now. Anything you want to add before I go to sleep?

Jesus: *I love you, and I'll be there with you when you dream.*

Day 2:

I see that Jesus would lean back, open His arms and cloak wide, and invite me to cuddle. His gift for me is to feel His love increasingly. His promise is that we will get through this leg of my journey together.

Me: Jesus, Your answer is clear, but short. Would You care to elaborate? What do You want me to ask You?

Jesus: *Ask Me why My cloak is grey.*

Me: Okay. Jesus, why is Your cloak grey?

Jesus: *Because I am gentle and humble in heart. I am humble like you— not much to look at in the eyes of this world—but I have a rich inner life with the Father. I wear this cloak when I am around you because I can be*

221

Myself with you. You're comfortable to be around, and I don't have to come in pomp and glory for you to see Me. We can rest, hidden from the world, together.

Me: Jesus, I feel as if I really am unimportant, because I am unable to do the things You have put into my heart and mind to do. I feel very frustrated by my body.

Jesus: *I understand. There was so much more that I wanted to do when I came in the flesh than My flesh allowed Me to do. You see from God's perspective some of the time—I see from it all of the time! Imagine how much more I wanted to give than I could! As I said before, you understand Me, and that's why I can be Myself around you. Do you have any idea how frustrating it is for people to want My glory, and not My humility? My work, not My rest? As I said before, I desire humility [mercy], not sacrifice (Hos 6:6; Matt 9:13). Put another way, I want relationship, not works. I love spending time with you and with others. Yes, you have physical limitations, but those limitations have enabled you to get to know Me in ways that not everyone takes the time for. Remember Matthew 7:22-23.*

Me: Jesus, when I heard, "Do you have any idea how frustrating it is for people to want My glory, and not My humility?" it sounded a bit harsh to me. Can You really feel frustrated? Do You really feel this way, or am I projecting my own paradigms and emotions onto You?

Jesus: *I feel really sad when people do not come to Me. My greatest desire is to talk with people, to spend time with them, to relate. I hunger and thirst to interact with My children. Do you remember the overwhelming joy you feel after you teach a group of people how to hear My voice, or do prophetic evangelism? That's My joy! I love it when you set up a meeting between Me and My children, and teach them how to have a conversation with Me on their own. I love it!*

Me: Jesus, is there anything else You want to tell me?

Jesus: *Not tonight. We'll talk more tomorrow. I love you.*

Murray's Entry

There are many ways that God speaks; therefore, it may be good to have some examples of these different ways, so we can "catch God in the act." I am going to do an activation myself, so you can have a journal example in which I break down the parts of the interaction I am having to show its feeling, thoughts, pictures, and flow while I write. That way, when God speaks in your own journal entries, you will be aware of what you are experiencing, and catch God in the act yourself.

Murray Journal for Week 41: My Place or Yours

I am sitting in my office and I think that if I could pick a place for Jesus to meet me, it would be right here, right now.

Q: Jesus, where would you like to meet me?

I have a sense of a mountaintop. I can't see it, but I know in my knower that is the place. As I ponder this sense, I get a sense of sitting at a picnic table with the Lord in a field. He is writing in a book, and I am sitting across from Him, also writing in a book. Again, at this point, I don't see this clearly, but I can now draw the picture in detail.

I am pondering how a picnic bench and field would be on top of a mountain. As I do this, suddenly I just know that the mountaintop represents meeting the Lord in a place of clear vision, and seeing a long way. The picnic table means sharing thoughts together. The books represent Him writing down His thoughts. As He writes his thoughts, I write down those same thoughts in my book. I intuitively know as I ponder with Him that we are sharing a picnic of His heavenly thoughts together.

Suddenly the picture becomes very clear, and I am seeing it on the inside of my eyelids. Jesus stands up, shakes His binder in the air, and all of the pages He has been writing on fall out, turn into white doves, and fly away into the sky. [I was pretty shocked when that happened.]

Jesus turns to me and wants me to do the same thing. I feel hesitant—I like my notes in my binder.

Journaling [going with the flow in writing at this point]: Jesus, I think I understand the setting, but why did You do that with what You wrote? You put a lot of time into writing that at the table with me.

Jesus: *I want to share it with the world; I want to get it out there. The doves represent My Spirit taking what is Mine and releasing it to My Bride, the church.*

Murray: I feel hesitant to do the same with my binder.

Jesus: *Why do you think that is?*

Murray: I am not sure I want to know! Lol! [I write that for you to be aware as God digs in our hearts, we are not always sure of what we are going to find, and that is pretty normal, at least for me.]

At this point, I sense Jesus looking at me, smiling. He is not letting me off the hook.

As I ponder how I feel I get a picture of a sonar device sending out its little sound wave to ping off of something, and of that wave coming back, allowing the sonar operator to know something else is out there. I feel like that. What if I send out my material and nothing happens? What if it makes no difference at all? Then what? I think that is what is making me feel hesitant.

Jesus: *What was the look on My face when I let My pages go?*

Murray: Exuberant joy!

Jesus: *I was modeling that joy for you! Look at how much fun it was for Me to just throw it all in the air, like seeds being carried by the wind, and see where all the pages could go! Let Me teach you that joy, My son. Throw your pages out there and see what happens.*

This is all pretty personal, but these back and forth encounters with the Lord often are. Isn't that the point? God wants to be personal. This is all about Ephesians 1:3-17, the purpose of revelation being to know who we are in Christ (Eph 1:3-14), and who God is for us in the midst of life (Eph 1:17-18). As you journal, don't be afraid to talk to God about deep things. If you feel deep emotions come up in your heart, look at the expression on the Lord's face and ask Him why He is looking at you that way while you feel what you are feeling. Allow the Lord to go deep with you. It may comforting to know it took me about two weeks to figure out why I couldn't throw my pages in the air. There were some fears and concerns I needed to look at in my heart. Then, finally, I could "let go," and my pages turned into doves and starting zooming around just like the Lords! (Thank you, Jesus! Being able to let go and trust you is a beautiful thing.)

One last thought about the above journal entry: notice how my entry started out with me not seeing much. I *felt* a picture, if that makes sense. But, as I got past thoughts of, "I am making this up," "That's what I want to see," etc., the pictures and interactions got clearer. As you work through this journal, this will happen for you as well: you will sense more clearly, hear more clearly, and picture more clearly.

Bless you all on your journey through *On Things Above*.

Other Resources from Samuel's Mantle

iDream Series

Do you believe God speaks through dreams?
Did you know that dreams can be a meeting place where you can talk with Jesus?
Did you know that dreams can be a beginning of a conversation?

iDream 1st Encounter – Journey in Dreaming

Topics:

- Why would God use dreams?
- Division of soul & spirit
- Dreams throughout history
- Remembering dreams
- Impartation to dream
- Keeping a dream journal
- God's secret dream language
- Eyes of the heart and dream work
- Testing revelation
- Emotions in a dream

iDream 2nd Encounter – 15 Different Ways to Interpret a Dream

Topics:

- Dream types & clues to which type you are dreaming
- Breaking down the dream cast – objects, actions, people, animals, settings
- Dramatic scene changes & life decisions
- Working with emotions
- Dream group model
- Discovering the 'click' moment

- Stepping into the dream
- Definition of terms
- Waking and living – discovering life changes from dreams, visions, signs & wonders

iDream 3rd Encounter – Developing Personal Growth Directions through Dreamwork

Topics:

- Dream types part 2
- Working with the anointing given by God in dreams
- Stepping into growth directions
- Dealing with nightmares
- Learning to be 'awake in your sleep'
- Developing your personal glossary
- Interacting with the Lord & angels in dreams

iDream series is available in CD or MP3 format, at www.samuelsmantle.com.

www.samuelsmantle.com

To order resources (books/cds/dvds) email

books@samuelsmantle.com

ALSO BY
MURRAY DUECK

If This Were A Dream What Would It Mean?

Discovering the Spiritual Meaning Behind Everyday Events.

Have you ever felt like God was trying to tell you something?

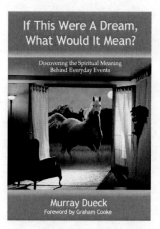

Perhaps you dreamt about someone you hadn't seen in a while and then ran into that person the following day. Maybe a strange story on the evening news grabbed your attention, putting you in a state of pondering. Or perhaps you encountered an odd sight like the one on the cover of this book that made you wonder if something was up.

If you can identify with any of the above, chances are you have already been in language school-God's symbolic language school! Just as Jesus taught his disciples to see the spiritual and symbolic meanings behind everyday events, God has also been urging you to interpret life on a symbolic level, asking, "If this were a dream what would it mean?"

In this book, author Murray Dueck helps you to develop your spiritual eyes, enabling you to glimpse the Kingdom of Heaven shining through everyday life. After reading this book, you will be able to:

- Encounter God in the routine events of life
- See God at work in your church, community, and world
- Pray according to what you see the Father doing
- Know beyond a shadow of a doubt that God-not the enemy-is in control of your life

www.samuelsmantle.com

Keepers of the Presence

Are you aware of divine moments?

It's an ordinary Sunday morning church service. Suddenly, the atmosphere changes—the presence of God has come!

Are you one of those who can sense or feel such divine moments? If so, then it's time for you to recognize the special calling God has given you. Some signs of your calling include the ability to

- sense if God's presence is released or hindered;

- know how people are feeling;

- sense or feel whether meetings or places are spiritually safe or troubled.

Keepers of the Presence is your roadmap to help you develop your unique gift of spiritual sensitivity so you can steward the presence of God wherever you go!

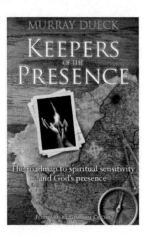

In this book you will find over 50 "Filling Stations" or activations designed to help you understand all that you sense and feel happening in the world around you. With these practical activities, you will discover how to respond appropriately and how to step into and release the presence of God.

www.samuelsmantle.com

ABOUT THE AUTHOR

Murray Dueck is the founder of Samuel's Mantle prophetic training school in the Vancouver area of British Columbia. For the past fourteen years, Murray has been teaching people how to interact with their heavenly Father by learning to listen to the Lord's voice through the myriad of ways God speaks: sensing/feeling, pictures, vision, dreams, prophecy, journaling, etc.

It is Murray's desire that people would intimately know their heavenly Father, and that takes communication. As much as not communicating or understanding our spouse affects our marriage relationship—so does not understanding the many ways God speaks affect our intimate relationship with Him. Consequently, it has been Murray's passion to introduce people to these many varied, and often personal, ways God reveals himself.

Writing is another of Murray's passions. He believes that settling down with a good book, letting the world slip by, and listening to the Lord's voice all at the same time, is time well spent. Murray's first book *If This Were a Dream What Would it Mean?* was his first attempt to have people disappear with the Lord between the pages of a book, and it went well enough to have another crack at it with *Keepers of the Presence.*

When not teaching or writing Murray enjoys spending time with his wife Kelly and his three teenagers Jesse, Delci, and Simeon just being silly, making up amusing songs, and singing off-key. At the end of the day, Murray spends time with his cat Fitzimpen (Fitzy for short) trying to discern what is on her mind. So far he has had no success.

ABOUT
SAMUEL'S MANTLE

Samuel's Mantle is a prophetic training school, dedicated to seeing the truth of Joel 2 lived out by Christians everywhere.

> *I will pour out my Spirit on all people. Your sons and daughters will prophesy, your old men will dream dreams, your young men will see visions. Even on my servants, both men and women, I will pour out my Spirit in those days. I will show wonders in the heavens and on earth. (Joel 2:28-29)*

Led by Murray and Kelly Dueck, Samuel's Mantle offers three levels of prophetic training classes aimed at equipping the Body of Christ to hear God speak and understand the many ways our Father communicates with us. Local classes run from Sept. to June.

Samuel's Mantle classes are also available online in video or audio, to download, or as CDs or DVDs. They can be ordered separately or as a group. This is a great way to start your own Samuel's Mantle class in your home town, or connect with others doing the course online. You can find us on Facebook under Samuel's Mantle Online.

Digital Delivery of Classes

For more details on these and other prophetic training resources, or to find out how you can get involved with Samuel's Mantle, please visit www.samuelsmantle.com.

Manufactured by Amazon.ca
Acheson, AB

13277084R00129